# SUCCESSFUL BEGINNINGS FOR COLLEGE TEACHING:

## Engaging Your Students from the First Day

by Angela Provitera McGlynn

Atwood Publishing
Madison, WI

Successful Beginnings for College Teaching:
Engaging Your Students from the First Day

by Angela Provitera McGlynn

Copyright © 2001 by Atwood Publishing

Volume 2, Teaching Techniques/Strategies Series

2710 Atwood Avenue

Madison, WI 53704

Printed in the United States of America

ISBN: 1-891859-38-2

Cover and text design TLC Graphics, www.tlcgraphics.com

Library of Congress Cataloguing-in-Publication Data

Provitera-McGlynn, Angela.
    Successful beginning for college teaching: engaging your students from the
first day/by Angela Provitera McGlynn
        p.cm. — (Teaching techniques/strategies series ; v.2)
    Includes bibliographical references.
    ISBN 1-891859-38-2
    1. College teaching. 2. College teachers. I.Title. II. Series.

LB2331 .P768 2001
378.1'25—dc21
                                                                2001053404

# DEDICATION

At the heart of all the blessings of my life are my parents, Ann and Joseph Provitera, whose gifts to me are innumerable. I am grateful most especially for their love, and then for their guidance, support, and for their faith in me. This book is also dedicated to my husband, Bruce McGlynn, my beloved partner for my whole adult life — a man whose capacity for loving and caring and having fun has made the journey so much more fulfilling.

# ACKNOWLEDGMENTS

Thank you ...

... to all of my students through all of my years of teaching, from whom I have learned so much. In my three decades in the college classroom, I have taught approximately four hundred students per year— about twelve thousand students in all!

... to my parents, who taught me the value of education, along with so many other pieces of wisdom that have sustained me through life.

... to my husband, my partner in life, who encourages my work, keeps me laughing, and always brings me joy.

... to my colleagues at Mercer County Community College, many of whom are also cherished friends, for their support, their sharing of ideas, their help with this project, and their caring about students and about teaching. Thanks especially to Patricia Carr for use of her work, *Passport to Success*, and for her decades-long friendship.

... to Bob Rosania, who has been like a brother to me, for giving me tips about writing this book as well as lifelong encouragement, love, and support.

... to Marilyn Gilroy, a dear friend and mentor, who helped with this writing project as well as many others.

... to Vera Goodkin, whose dedicated study of the role of writing in learning has inspired me as a teacher and as a writer.

... to Carolyn Del Monte and Laura Ingersoll, whose kind help in locating references for this book facilitated my research.

... to Marta Kaufmann, whose kind guidance helped get this project off the ground floor.

... to Tom Wilfrid, Vice President of Mercer County Community College, and Andy Conrad, my division dean, who have both supported me in so many academic endeavors, including the writing of this book.

... to Peter Vogt, the creative, kind, and masterful editor of this book, whose guidance, insights, and editorial skills were top-notch.

... to Linda Babler, the publisher of this book, whose vision is responsible for making this book a reality.

*Angela Provitera McGlynn*
2001

# TABLE OF CONTENTS

Teach Students to Do Well in Your Course
Make Your Attendance Policy Clear
Gather Information about Your Students
Accommodate Students Who Have Special Needs
Some Ideas on Promoting Student Success
Clarify Your Testing Policy
The Issue of Academic Integrity
Some Quick Tips on Managing the Learning Environment
Guidelines for Student Success (handout)
Preparing for and Taking Exams (handout)
More Tips for Test Preparation and Test Taking (handout)

Family Name Exercise
"What's in a Name?" Exercise
Stand Up-Sit Down Exercise
Activities That Help Students Find Commonalities
Introduction by Identities Exercise
Student Disclosure Exercises
    Dyadic interviews

# INTRODUCTION

I believe that teaching is an art. As in any art, it takes plenty of practice to hone your skills as a teacher. Practice alone, however, won't make you an *effective* teacher. If it did, we wouldn't have all those teachers who stay in the profession for years and years and yet don't seem to get any better at their craft.

So, in addition to practice, effective teaching takes some good direction with respect to what works in the classroom. College teaching is unique in that preparing for it involves mastering a discipline but not necessarily learning the art of teaching. That's why I've written this book — to give you some guidance in the art of teaching, especially as it relates to getting your classes off to a productive start that establishes a positive, learning conducive classroom atmosphere for the entire semester.

If you're a graduate student interested in pursuing college teaching, a teaching assistant, an adjunct instructor, or a new full-time faculty member, I hope this book will provide you with some of the tools that are essential for becoming an effective teacher, from "Day 1" of each of your classes. Becoming an effective teacher is not about achieving a goal and then stopping. Rather, it's about continually evolving, constantly trying new strategies, and always striving to do better. For that reason, I expect that veteran teachers will benefit from this book too.

I wrote this book at this particular point in time because I believe we need to develop new teaching strategies to reach our changing college student populations. If you're teaching at an Ivy League institution, for example, you'll probably be teaching students who are not only very bright and well prepared for college-level work, but who are also highly motivated to learn, to do well, and to achieve. Throughout the rest of mainstream colleges and universities — especially at community, commuter, and urban institutions — you'll be working with many students who lack the educational preparedness to be successful in college. Particularly at community and commuter colleges, many of your students will be juggling work schedules and family responsibilities in addition to their course loads. Many of these students will need to learn *how* to learn; they'll need to develop study skills and organizational and time-management skills, and they may need to make up for reading, writing, and mathematical deficiencies before they can even start college-level coursework. If you teach (or will be teaching) at such an institution, you'll need to develop teaching skills that go far beyond delivering a well-thought-out, thorough, and interesting set of lectures.

College teaching can be a pretty isolating experience. I'm fortunate to be at a college where my colleagues and I have many opportunities to talk about what's happening in our classes. Many of us who eat lunch together use our time to discuss what has worked well in our classes, and sometimes we share what has bombed as well. Often, one of us will pose a problem he or she is dealing with and the rest of us will try to strategize and offer solutions. In addition to lunchtime conversation, we also have some grassroots groups that meet on a monthly basis to discuss some aspect of teaching. For example, we have a committee called Writing Across the Disciplines (WAD) that meets to explore how we can enhance the writing and oral communication skills of our students. We also have a group known as the Mercer Curriculum Project (MCP), which I chair, which aims to transform the curriculum in terms of inclusiveness, and to create a more welcoming classroom atmosphere. In addition, we have a group called Master Faculty that meets to share the trials and tribulations of teaching. Some meetings have the feeling of group therapy. At other times, we observe each other in the classroom, not for purposes of evaluation but simply as a way to enhance our own teaching skills.

All of these groups are voluntary and apart from our duties related to college governance. My friends and colleagues at other institutions tell me that what we have going at my college, in terms of collegial sharing about teaching, is pretty rare. My suggestion to you as you start or continue to develop in this profession is that you connect with your colleagues and talk about teaching. Without the back-and-forth dialogue, it's easy to feel like you're all alone.

My hope for *Successful Beginnings* is that it will help you become a more effective teacher and promote student success. As the title of the book suggests, I believe that the early part of the semester is crucial for setting a tone that motivates your students to persist in your course. If students drop a course, they're most likely to drop it in the first six weeks of the term. So to improve our retention rates — and thus give ourselves a chance to teach students what we want them to learn — we must be effective from Day 1.

In this book, you'll learn how to get your course off to a positive, fruitful start so that your students will be motivated to participate and engaged in their learning right from the very start. I begin in Chapter 1 by covering "The Nuts and Bolts of Successful Beginnings" — making your expectations clear, creating a welcoming classroom environment, and helping students thrive in your classroom.

Chapter 2 describes some innovative activities you can use in the first couple of class sessions to "break the ice," learn students' names (and help them learn each others' names), and set a productive tone for the rest of the semester. After your first class, you want your students to look forward to coming back for the next session ... and the next ... and the next.

Chapter 3 explores how you can create a welcoming, inclusive classroom environment. I present some research about "The Chilly Classroom Climate." This is a phrase coined to denote the differential treatment of females and other "minority" groups in schools at all levels. In order to create an atmosphere in which **all** students feel welcomed, included, and encouraged, I offer tips in this chapter for building rapport and connecting with students. I also discuss strategies that promote student-student interaction.

Chapter 4 is all about motivating your students, especially the ones who seem disengaged. Here I offer suggestions for getting your students to become *self-regulators* — that is, helping them take charge of their own learning. I also outline some tips on teaching your students *how* to learn and how to improve their own learning skills. Chapter 4 also points out ways to make your classes more interactive. Most educators agree that students learn more and retain more when they're actively involved. Thus, this chapter is designed to help you raise the level of student participation in your classes. I deal with how to make your lectures more interactive, how to improve the quality of your classroom discussions and bring more people into them, and how to create and implement *collaborative* and *cooperative* learning experiences.

Earlier I mentioned the changing nature of our national college student body. Something else has changed in the last few decades at our colleges and universities: the college culture itself. Students' expectations and demands have changed. There is a new "consumer" mentality; some students believe that, because they're paying for the course, they get to run the show. What we as teachers used to take for granted in terms of college student behavior can no longer be taken for granted. Although the majority of our students are respectful of their teachers and honest in the work they produce, there are some students who simply don't know what is appropriate behavior for the college classroom – or perhaps they choose not to follow the conventions. So Chapter 5 helps you take on the challenge of dealing with *incivility* in the classroom. I hope the suggestions throughout this book, and from this chapter in particular, will promote a classroom climate that is not conducive to incivility. There are many things we can do as teachers to prevent inappropriate and disruptive behavior from occurring in the first place, and I talk about them in Chapter 5 — along with what you can do if disruptive behavior does occur.

Chapter 6 addresses the challenge of keeping students engaged during the "mid-semester blahs," and suggests ways to motivate them to complete your course successfully. Additionally, I discuss the role of writing in keeping students engaged with the course, and in promoting learning and critical thinking. I also describe some active learning exercises that will help you keep students "hooked," and a few closing exercises to foster retention of the course material and help students achieve a sense of completion as the course draws to a close.

Finally, in Chapter 7, I summarize the material the book has covered. Following that closing chapter you'll find a brief Appendix offering you guidance and resources if you're developing a course syllabus — especially if you're doing so for the first time. A "Helpful Teaching Resources" section then highlights some books, periodicals, web sites, professional organizations, and professional conferences that will help you in all of your efforts to create positive learning experiences for your students — right from the start of each class you teach.

My hunch is that if you're a college teacher, or you're about to become one, you love your discipline, because you're choosing to share it with others. I believe that anyone who chooses college teaching is interested in helping students develop critical thinking skills and become intellectually curious. My own observations of teachers have led me to believe that most of us feel as if we have a vocation, a special calling to make a difference in the world by educating people. There is nobility in teaching. Heaven knows people don't aspire to become college teachers for money! We don't usually get rich in this profession. But we do enrich the lives of others, and thus we find rewards that are far deeper and more meaningful.

To quote the abstract of Thomas Cronin's (1992, 149) article, "On Celebrating College Teaching":

> Great teachers give us a sense not only of who they are, but more important, of who we are, and who we might become. They unlock our energies, our imaginations, and our minds. Effective teachers pose compelling questions, explain options, teach us to reason, suggest possible directions, and urge us on. The best teachers, like the best leaders, have an uncanny ability to step outside themselves and become liberating forces in our lives.

Good luck on your journey. I hope this book is helpful to you.

CHAPTER ONE

# CLASSROOM
# AND COURSE MANAGEMENT:
## The Nuts and Bolts of Successful Beginnings

## Teach Students
## to Do Well in Your Course

At the very beginning of the semester, it's a good idea to discuss the types of study habits and strategies students will need to succeed in your course. This approach is particularly helpful if you're teaching an introductory course that has many first-year students. Sitting in our classes are many students who are underprepared to do college work. Many of them don't have basic skills that we once took for granted as part of college preparation. They may not write well, they may have reading difficulties, and they may not know how to use a library. They may not have well-developed study skills, time management skills, or organizational skills. This may not be true for students at our selective Ivy League institutions, but it is certainly true of many students in our community and urban institutions and in the rest of higher education. So you may want to give your students a handout with some tips for their success. I've included one ("Guidelines for Student Success") at the end of this chapter that you may use or adapt.

You might feel there isn't enough time to teach your course's content *and* teach your students how to do well in your course. That's certainly understandable. But rest assured that the "payoffs" from your investment will more than compensate for the time you spend. Turner (1999) believes that student retention and success in college are linked to introducing students to academic citizenship. What this means is that, as an instructor, you may need to take class time to explain fundamental information you might never have had to explain in the past. Turner says we must tell our students that they need to buy the book required for the course, read the assignments and attend classes, meet deadlines or make special arrangements when doing so is impossible, and so on. We as faculty also need to develop a mindset about our emerging roles as college teachers. Instead of staying rooted in the old tradition of seeing ourselves as delivery systems of information in our disciplines, we need to instead view ourselves as "teachers of students."

Needless to say, our task at this point in time is more challenging than it has been in the past. Effective teachers guide their students from the level the *students* start at, directing them to the resources they'll need to succeed, motivating them to achieve, and challenging them to develop. For college teachers committed to maintaining academic standards, this task of starting where the student is "at" and moving forward from there is challenging indeed. The rewards of doing so, however, are all the more magnified. When we see our students move from taking developmental math and reading classes to successfully completing calculus and a literature course, we reap the rewards of our efforts. Then we know that these students, who started at a pre-college level, have progressed to mastering advanced college-level work.

One of my colleagues reads to students the comments and tips of her previous semester's students about how to do well in her course. Students are often more impressed by the wisdom of fellow students who have been through the course than by the suggestions of their instructors.

I often tell my students that many educators, including my colleagues at the college, believe that students who sit in the front of the classroom seem to be more engaged in the course, and are, therefore, more successful. I also give students tips about notetaking. I start by talking about how people learn through a variety of means, but then I build a case for notetaking. I talk about how the process of taking notes keeps people more tuned in to what's being discussed. I add that taking notes is a way to learn the material, since organizing and writing are ways we encode information to be stored in our memories. And then I jokingly tell the students that even if it's not true that writing helps them to remember, if they forget what they've written at least they'll have a record they can use to review and study.

I allow students to tape classes if they want to. This accommodation is particularly helpful to students who have perceptual and learning differences, for whom notetaking doesn't work very well. However, I caution students that taping the class may have some downsides. I suggest that it may, for instance, make it easier for them to "tune out" of the class session.

I add that listening to the tape later in the day is quite time consuming when compared to simply reading over one's notes.

As instructors, we need to think through our courses so that we know what the ingredients are for success. For example, in my introductory psychology course — and I'm sure this is true in most courses — one of the critical variables for success is that students not fall behind. This is the type of tip that students take to heart more if they hear it from previous students and not me.

# Make Your Attendance Policy Clear

In addition to including your attendance policy on your course syllabus (see the Appendix if you want/need tips on developing an effective syllabus), it helps to talk about the policy when you hand your syllabus out. I'm aware of the arguments against formulating attendance policies. Some of my colleagues believe it's the student's responsibility to attend class. They argue that, since our students are adults and are paying tuition for the courses they take, they have the right to make their own decisions about class attendance.

Although I understand and can agree with this position philosophically, my teaching experience has led me to create and emphasize an attendance policy. I've found that students are more inclined to attend class if I take roll in every class and if there are some cost/reward consequences tied to their attendance. In my syllabus, the wording of my attendance policy (as well as my late-to-class policy and my policies concerning late exams and late papers) includes the phrase "*may result* in a point reduction or the lowering of a grade." That way I'm not bound to penalize a student. I like to keep my options open for students who have special circumstances. Many more-mature, returning adult students may need even more leeway than our traditional-age students.

When I tell the students about my attendance policy, I provide a rationale for it. I tell them that one of the key factors in student success in college is class attendance. I also tell them that what happens in class is unique and is not easily replaced by copying someone else's notes or reading the textbook.

Although some of my students complain about the policy, the great majority of them tell me informally, in focus groups, or on course evaluations that the policy is an additional incentive that motivates them to come to class.

An occasional reminder of the policy during the semester is helpful too. One of my colleagues offers an award at the end of the term for perfect attendance. She announces the award on the first day of class and mentions that, in addition to motivation and perseverance, never missing a class involves a certain amount of luck as well. In her last class of the semester, which is an award ceremony, there is often more than one recipient of the "perfect attendance" award. My colleague usually gives out small academic pocket calendars/planners. You may want to create certificates, give books, or hand out some other small token, depending on how many recipients you have.

## Gather Information about Your Students

In your first or second class period, you might want to have your students fill out index cards with their names, the courses they've taken in your discipline, their phone numbers, their e-mail addresses, and the hours they can be reached. You can say that you might want to reach them at some point during the semester; most students don't feel intruded upon by this request. Instead, they feel cared about.

Wolcowitz (1984) suggests several pieces of student information that you may request on index cards. For example, you can ask your students what year they are in college to get a sense of their assimilation to the college environment and to college-level expectations. You might also want to know your students' fields of concentration, so that you can better understand the role of your course in your students' programs of study. You may want to know what other courses the students have taken in your discipline or in related fields; this will give you a sense of the students' familiarity with major concepts and modes of analysis in your discipline. For certain courses, you may want to know the extent of the students' math and English backgrounds. You may be interested in what other courses the student is currently taking. You might also want to ask your students why they're taking your course; doing so will give you a sense of their expectations for the course, and will allow you to discuss what the course will cover and whether the students' expectations are on target. In some cases, if you have some leeway in your course, you may even be able to modify what you had planned in order to meet the goals of your students.

I often ask students to write on the backs of their cards anything about themselves that they would like to share with me. I invite them to give me any hints about teaching/learning strategies that work well for them. Students often take the opportunity to explain to me their learning disabilities, and to share strategies they have successfully used to compensate for them.

# Accommodate Students
# Who Have Special Needs

Early in the semester, some of your students may give you an "accommodations" form, stating that they have been diagnosed with a learning disability and describing what accommodations would be helpful to them. Although there is ongoing debate about the meaning of "learning disabilities," most definitions would suggest that a *learning disability* refers to a disorder that affects how an individual with normal or above-average intelligence processes information, stores information, or expresses information.

There is usually a deficit between the student's potential for learning and what he or she actually learns. Deficits may occur in one or more of the following areas:

- oral expression,
- written expression,
- listening comprehension,
- basic reading skills,
- reading comprehension,
- mathematical calculation, or
- problem solving.

Students with learning disabilities may also have difficulty with sustained attention, time management, and/or social skills. There is general agreement that a learning disability is not a form of mental retardation or an emotional disorder. However, one emotional problem that most students with learning disabilities face, at least at first, is frustration. Learning disabilities have often been referred to as "hidden" disabilities, since the disability itself isn't readily visible to others. Once a student has self-disclosed his or her disability, handle the student and the self-disclosure with a caring sensibility.

Be sure to familiarize yourself with your institution's policies concerning accommodations and introduce yourself to the college's learning disabilities specialists. You must follow policy, since your institution is probably bound to meet the requirements of the Americans with Disabilities Act (ADA).

Students are sometimes embarrassed by their disabilities and feel awkward about bringing them to your attention. As faculty, we need to be sensitive to our students' feelings and special needs. Usually, the accommodations they request are fairly easy to abide by, such as granting permission for students to tape lectures or take extra time for exams. We should be impressed with the perseverance these students have — they've made it to college despite some extra difficulties in their paths.

Brinckerhoff (1991) says that, as faculty members, we can play a critical role in the lives of students who may have *undiagnosed* learning disabilities — by referring them to a trained specialist. So we may find ourselves not only responding to students who self-disclose, but also playing some role in the *identification* of students with learning disabilities. Once these students are identified, we can help them develop academic accommodations and adjustments that will allow them to fully access the course material.

Brinckerhoff (1991) offers the following tips that we as faculty can use to help students with learning disabilities. You'll notice that many of these suggestions are good teaching strategies that will work well with *all* students:

- Encourage students to make an appointment during office hours to self-disclose any learning disabilities they might have. Ask students who identify themselves how you, as a teacher, can help them best learn course material.
- Provide students with a detailed course syllabus. If possible, make it available before registration week.
- Clearly spell out your course expectations (regarding grading, material to be covered, due dates, etc.) before the course begins.
- Start each lecture with an outline of the material to be covered that period. At the conclusion of the class, briefly summarize your key points.
- Speak directly to your students, and use gestures and natural expressions to convey further meaning.
- Present new or technical vocabulary on the blackboard or in a handout. Use new terms in context to best convey their meaning.
- Give assignments both orally and in writing to avoid confusion.
- Announce reading assignments well in advance for students who are using taped materials. It takes an average of four weeks to get a book tape-recorded.
- If possible, select a textbook with an accompanying study guide for optional student use.
- Provide adequate opportunities for questions and answers, including review sessions.
- Allow students to record lectures to facilitate their notetaking.

- Provide, in advance, study questions for exams that illustrate the format and content of the test. Explain what constitutes a good answer and why.

- If necessary, allow students with learning disabilities to demonstrate mastery of course material using alternative methods (e.g., extended time limits for testing, oral exams in a separate room).

- Permit use of simple calculators, scratch paper, pocket spellers, and dictionaries during exams (no programmable calculators, though!).

- Encourage students to use campus support services — for example, pre-registration, assistance in ordering taped textbooks, alternative testing arrangements, specialized study aids, peer support groups, diagnostic consultation, study skills seminars, developmental skills courses, and academic tutorial assistance.

## Some Ideas
## on Promoting Student Success

Here's another teaching tip that may contribute to student success, not only for students with learning disabilities but for all of our students: At the beginning of each class session, ask for a student volunteer to summarize the main points of the last class. This provides continuity and a starting point for the students who were there, and fills in the missing pieces for students who were absent. It also reinforces one of our goals as teachers: To help students feel comfortable with oral communication.

Then, announce the topics you'll be covering and your objectives for the day's session. Give your students a preview of what you plan to accomplish. The old adage, "Tell them what you're going to tell them, tell them, and then tell them what you told them" seems to be quite an effective teaching strategy.

Some teachers write an outline for the day on the blackboard. If you use this tool, mention where you are on your outline as the class session unfolds. In doing so, you'll establish checkpoints where you can recap and give students an opportunity to ask or answer questions.

Other teachers use a *minute paper* during or following a class session to assess whether students have understood the material presented. Two questions for a minute paper seem to suffice: 1) "What is the most important thing you learned in class today?" and 2) "What is the main, unanswered question you leave class with today?" (Angelo and Cross 1993, 148-153). The minute paper is the most well-known of the *classroom as-*

*sessment techniques* (CATs). "Classroom assessment," which is practiced through the use of classroom assessment techniques, was introduced in the late 1980s by Cross (1986) and Cross and Angelo (1988). The basic assumption is that we as teachers need to know what our students are learning and how they're responding to our teaching strategies. We can use these classroom assessment techniques across the disciplines to assess our students' learning during the term, while there's still time to change and adjust our instructional approaches.

Assessments such as the minute paper are teaching tools in addition to learning assessment strategies. The minute paper, for example, engages students in monitoring their own learning by asking them to think about what they've learned, articulate it in writing, and critically examine what they didn't understand. As a teacher, you can read these anonymous assessments to get a better handle on the current level of the class. Remember, too, that the approach also offers a non-threatening way to get students to disclose what material they find confusing.

# Clarify
# Your Testing Policy

Be sure to clearly explain your philosophy and purposes in testing both in the course syllabus and in your early-semester classes. Create exams that focus on the most important topics covered in the text and in your class sessions. Students appreciate instructors who provide study guidelines and/or objectives booklets to help them navigate through the material.

Find a balance on the frequency of your testing so that you cover a reasonable amount of material on each exam. The traditional college model of a midterm exam, a final exam, and a paper no longer works well with today's college students. They want more inputs into their final grade, and more opportunities for testing so that they can more readily manage the quantity of material to be learned. Some creative teachers even find ways to engage students in the creation of tests so that the students feel empowered and more connected to the course.

You might also want to offer your students some basic tips for test taking. At the end of this chapter you'll find two sample handouts — "Preparing for and Taking Exams" and "More Tips for Test Preparation and Test Taking" — which you may want to use or adapt for your students.

Create the first test of the course to cover a smaller amount of material than the later exams will. Often, students are just getting their feet wet and attempting to learn the language of your discipline in the first few weeks of the semester. Their first test experience, then, should boost their confidence and motivate them to persevere. Explain in advance what your exams will cover and how they'll be graded. Remind students of your grading policies occasionally during the semester when you're helping them prepare for an exam or a paper, and when you're returning exams and papers to them. Review material before exams and follow up after returning tests.

It's very important to return graded tests and papers to students as soon as possible. Learning theorists tell us that the closer the feedback to the learning experience (the test or paper), the greater the reinforcement of the learned material. Additionally, students are usually anxious to get their work back. Prompt feedback helps keep them engaged with the course.

Offer constructive written feedback on exams and papers so that students will know how they can improve their work in the future. Usually, it helps to begin with positive statements about the student's *work*, and to then follow with specific suggestions for improvement. I emphasize the word "work" because many students take teachers' comments personally. Help your students realize that you (and their other instructors) are commenting on the quality of their performance on a specific task, and not on them as individuals.

# The Issue of Academic Integrity

You'll notice in my examples of course syllabi at the end of the Appendix ("Creating Your Course Syllabus: A Brief Overview") that each syllabus includes a statement on *academic integrity.* This statement, which comes from my own college's Academic Standards Committee, defines what academic integrity is and describes three violations of academic integrity. Many institutions have similar statements as part of their college policies.

The statement reads:

Academic integrity refers to the "integral" quality of the search for knowledge that a student undertakes. The work a student produces, therefore, ought to be wholly his or hers; it should result completely from the student's own efforts. A student will be guilty of violating academic integrity if he/she a) knowingly represents work of others as his/her own, b) uses or obtains unauthorized assistance in the execution of any academic work, or c) gives fraudulent assistance to another student.

Very recently, the Academic Standards Committee revised the policy so that it would be clearer and more detailed. See the revised policy statement (figure 1).

23

# ACADEMIC INTEGRITY POLICY

Mercer County Community College is committed to Academic Integrity — the honest, fair and continuing pursuit of knowledge, free from fraud or deception. This implies that students are expected to be responsible for their own work, and that faculty members will take reasonable precautions to prevent the opportunity for academic dishonesty.

The college recognizes the following general categories of violations of Academic Integrity, with representative examples of each. Academic Integrity is violated whenever a student:

A. Uses or obtains unauthorized assistance in any academic work.

- Copying from another student's exam.
- Using notes, books, or other aids of any kind during an exam when prohibited.
- Stealing an exam or possessing a stolen copy of an exam.

B. Gives fraudulent assistance to another student.

- Completing an academic activity or taking an exam for someone else.
- Giving answers to or sharing answers with another student during an exam.
- Sharing answers during an exam by using a system of signals.

C. Knowingly represents the work of others as his/her own, or represents previously completed academic work as current.

- Submitting a paper or another academic work, for credit, that includes words, ideas, data, or creative work of others without acknowledging the source.
- Using another author's words without enclosing them in quotation marks, without paraphrasing them, or without citing the source appropriately.
- Presenting another individual's work as one's own.
- Submitting the same paper or academic assignment to another class without the permission of the instructor.

D. Fabricates data in support of an academic assignment.

- Falsifying bibliographic entries.
- Submitting any academic assignment that contains falsified or fabricated data or results.

Figure 1: Academic Integrity Policy

E. Inappropriately or unethically uses technological means to gain academic advantage.

- Inappropriately or unethically acquiring material via the Internet.
- Using hidden devices for communication during an exam.
- Each instructor is authorized to establish specific guidelines consistent with this policy.

### Consequences for Violations of Academic Integrity

For a single violation, the faculty member will determine the course of action to be followed. This may include assigning a lower grade on the assignment, assigning a lower final course grade, failing the student in the course, or another penalty appropriate to the violation. In all cases, the instructor shall notify the chairperson of the Academic Standards Committee of the violation and the penalty imposed.

When two (or more) violations of Academic Integrity are reported on a student, the Academic Standards Committee may impose disciplinary penalties beyond those imposed by the course instructor(s). The student shall have the right to a hearing before the ASC or a designated subcommittee thereof.

### Appeals

The student has a right to appeal the decision of the instructor or of the Academic Standards Committee. Judicial procedures governing violations of Academic Integrity are contained in the Student Handbook.

Approved: Board of Trustees, May 18, 2000

**Figure 1: Academic Integrity Policy, con't**

The Academic Standards Committee at my college spells out the consequences of a violation but leaves the severity of the consequences up to the individual instructor. This is the case at many colleges and universities. Instructors often have to decide whether a student who "cheats" will receive a lower grade or failure on the particular assignment, or if he or she will instead fail the course altogether. Some institutions have a more severe penalty: Cheating results in dismissal from the school. If we believe the news reports of widespread cheating among high school and college students nationally, we need to learn to encourage academic honesty in our classes. Art Crawley, director of the Center for Faculty Development at Louisiana State University, believes that we as faculty should have a broad goal when thinking about fostering academic integrity. Crawley (2000) suggests that we should try to create a culture — what I would call a "classroom atmosphere" — favoring academic honesty and integrity. At the same time, we need to be prepared to deal with dishonest behaviors in our courses if and when they occur.

Crawley refers to ten principles of academic integrity proposed by McCabe and Pavela (1997). I see them as useful guidelines for creating a classroom atmosphere that promotes academic honesty. The principles:

1. *Affirm the importance of academic integrity.* An easy way to abide by this principle is to have in your course syllabus your institution's policy statement on academic honesty, and to reiterate your commitment to the institution's policy in one of your first classes of the semester. You may want to give students reminders about these standards before exams and when major projects are due.

2. *Foster a love of learning.* Throughout this book I emphasize the importance of showing enthusiasm for our disciplines and for learning. If our students "catch" our curiosity and excitement, they'll be more likely to do their own work. To help them stay on track, if you assign a paper, you might want to require that students submit an outline first, then a draft or notes on the paper, and then the final product. This process increases the probability that the student is doing his or her own work.

3. *Treat students as ends in themselves.* Here again, getting to know our students as individuals goes a long way toward encouraging them to be honest with us. If we show students respect by getting to know them and by working hard ourselves, they'll be more likely to respect us by being honest in their work. We also show students respect when our grading policies are fair and clear.

4. *Foster an environment of trust in the classroom.* Crawley says we create an atmosphere of trust when we make our standards clear and then adhere to those standards fairly.

5. *Encourage student responsibility for academic integrity.* If we ask students to work in small groups, we should have ways to assess individual contributions for group work. Sometimes, students may grade each other, or they may comment in writing on their own performance and that of their partners.

6. *Clarify expectations for students.* Crawley says this is one of the most important factors that can promote student academic honesty. Once again, the place for crystal clear explanations about policies and expectations concerning exams, group work, pa-

pers due, makeup exams and late papers, and grading is your course syllabus.

7. *Develop fair and relevant forms of assessment.* Having assessment tools that test what we say we want to measure is another way of establishing a trusting classroom climate.

8. *Reduce opportunities to engage in academic dishonesty.* Rather than facing the difficult task of penalizing transgressors of academic integrity, create a testing environment that makes it very difficult to cheat. This may involve seating arrangements that make it impossible to see another paper, the use of multiple forms of exams, or the creation of exams with scrambled questions.

9. *Challenge academic dishonesty when it occurs.* I am reminded of a dilemma I faced as a fairly new instructor. I was teaching a psychology course in a minimum-security prison for men. During an exam, two students engaged in one of the most obvious examples of cheating I have ever witnessed. These two young prisoners coughed loudly while dropping their exams on the floor. When they picked them up, they switched papers in my full view. As a young woman in a room full of inmates, I debated in my mind what to do. I summoned up my courage and simply walked up to them and asked them to switch back to their original exams. To this day, I don't know if I handled the situation in the best way. I was heartened at the time by the response of the students I had confronted. After the exam, they said they were glad that I had caught them cheating because at least now they would know what they really earned on the exam. Crawley says that if we don't challenge cheating when we see it, we're sending a message that contradicts our stated values. We also undermine the hard work and efforts of the majority of the students in our classes — the honest ones.

10. *Help define and support campus-wide integrity standards.* It is our responsibility to be campus role models of academic integrity, and to work with our institutions to create clear, well-defined academic standards policies and procedures.

Crawley argues that these ten principles, spelled out by McCabe and Pavela, can promote positive values and create a climate of trust and honesty: "The principles can serve as a good beginning for thinking about our roles, duties, and responsibilities as college and university teachers and scholars — as a community devoted to the pursuit of truth with integrity" (Crawley 2000, 7).

Johnson (1999, 5) suggests the following additional strategies to improve our teaching and prevent cheating among our students:

- *De-emphasize grades as much as possible.* Involve students in the evaluation of their own learning. Emphasize objective, non-judgmental feedback rather than A-B-C-D-F.

- *Emphasize your role in relation to the student* as colleague, coach, mentor, co-learner — one who orchestrates the resources rather than merely the expert. Experts are a dime a dozen; good teachers are rare.

- *Try to move beyond recall.* As quickly as possible, get students into analysis and synthesis.

- *Give take-home, open-book exams.* Encourage appropriate teamwork in learning. Use lots of small-group instruction, encouraging students to learn from each other, to cooperate rather than compete. Provide options in methodology. Perhaps some students would learn more doing a journal than a paper, or could profit by planning and conducting independent research.

- *Help students focus on their own learning.* Ask often and sincerely, "How do you know that?" "How did you learn that?" "What is your experience with this concept?" Help students to become learners, not only learned.

## Some Quick Tips on Managing the Learning Environment

Socializing your students in appropriate classroom behaviors in addition to academic honesty is critical to creating a positive learning environment from Day 1. The college classroom of today is quite different from the classroom of yesteryear. Some students are either unfamiliar with ordinary rules of decorum or choose not to follow them. In Chapter 5 ("Dealing with Incivility in the College Classroom"), I elaborate on a "Guidelines for Courtesy and Respect" handout that you may want to consider adopting for your course syllabus or as a separate resource. Although it may not have been necessary to discuss appropriate classroom behavior with college students in previous decades, it seems to be an essential factor these days at colleges and universities throughout the United States.

As manager of the classroom, you may sometimes feel you should know all the "answers." Many of us become masters at answering questions even when we're on shaky ground. Learn to feel comfortable admitting you don't know everything; doing so actually gives you greater credibility in students' eyes. Tell your students you'll research their questions, and then follow up with the research and with an answer(s), perhaps in the next class session.

Be sure as well to attend to factors that are relevant to the classroom learning experience, such as room temperature, air ventilation, and competing noise from outside the room. These are the kinds of mundane learning environment details that can make the difference between a good class session and a nonproductive one. If your classroom is hot and stuffy, you may very well find your students struggling to stay awake. Or if the noise from outside the room is competing with your class session, your students may not be able to attend to what's happening.

*Remember:* You're in charge of the *total* learning environment, right from the very start. It's up to you to create a "successful beginning" that will give you and your students the momentum you need to have a mutually positive teaching and learning experience. In Chapter 2, we begin discussing specific strategies and activities you can use to do just that.

# Guidelines for Student Success

To be successful in college, you'll need to be prepared, develop effective study skills, and manage your time productively.

## Be Prepared and Organized

- Buy the textbook and any accompanying supplements, such as workbooks and study guides, as soon as your course begins.
- Use a pocket calendar or an appointment book to keep track of your classes, assignments, due dates, work schedule, and any appointments you make with your instructors, counselors, or advisors.
- Use a notebook with pockets, a binder, or folders for your courses to have a place to take class notes, and to keep copies of your course syllabi, handouts, and any other pertinent materials.
- Always be prepared for class with pens and pencils, your notebook, and any other books required for class.
- It's helpful to carry around a good paperback college dictionary.

## Student Behavior That Contributes to Success

- Attend all of your classes and be on time.
- Read assigned material before class.
- Ask questions if you're not sure about assignments or the material covered.
- Show your interest in the subject by sitting near the front of the class, establishing eye contact with your instructor, and taking notes.
- Participate in class discussions.
- Avoid whispering or talking with classmates in side conversations while the instructor or another student has the floor.
- Complete your assignments on time.
- If you unavoidably miss a class, be responsible by informing your instructor; ask a classmate or your instructor what was covered, and make up the missed work.

Adapted from *Passport to Success*, by Patricia Anne Carr,
Mercer County Community College Press.

# Preparing for and Taking Exams

- Be sure about what material the exam will cover, and what type of questions (essay, multiple-choice, short-answer, matching) will be asked.

- Study from the beginning of the course, a little bit each day (Boyd 1988).

- Try to relate information to your own experience or to what you've previously learned. Chapter outlines and summaries will help you organize and remember the material.

- Study with a partner, or organize a small (three- or four-person) study group. Plan to meet after you've all studied the material individually so that you can compare notes and quiz each other.

- Use the proven effective "SQ3R" method of study. SQ3R stands for: **S**urvey, **Q**uestion, **R**ead, **R**ecite, and **R**eview. Lester A. Lefton (2000) adds "Write and Reflect" to this list and calls the approach the "SQ3R Plus System." Here's how the system works:

  - **S**urvey the chapter(s) you'll be tested on by paying attention to the chapter outlines, topic headings, tables, graphs, and other special features, particularly the summary and review sections.

  - Develop **Q**uestions based on topic headings within each chapter. In other words, change the topic headings into questions. This will help you become an active learner as you search for the answers.

  - **R**ead each chapter slowly and carefully and answer the questions you've posed. Take notes as you read and highlight key points. Make the material relevant to your personal life.

  - **R**ecite what you've learned from memory, putting the material into your own words.

  - **R**eview what you've learned. Try pulling together key terms and concepts. Check the accuracy of your recall by testing yourself.

  - Write and **R**eflect: Write a summary of the key terms and concepts in your own words and think about how they relate to your life. Lefton says that when you reflect on your own learning, you're an active learner and a critical thinker.

Adapted from Lefton (2000, 646a).

# More Tips for Test Preparation and Test Taking

Get a good night's sleep before the exam so that you can think clearly. Eat a healthy breakfast before taking a morning test. If your exam is in the afternoon or evening, make sure you're rested and that you haven't missed a meal.

- Always follow directions very carefully when you take an exam.
- Bring all the supplies you'll need to the test — e.g., pencils, pens, paper (Boyd 1988).
- Arrive early for the test.
- Try to relax. Take a few deep breaths, stay calm, and listen carefully to instructions.
- Budget your time so that you'll be able to complete the test.
- If time permits, go over your test to double-check your answers.
- Know how you'll be tested so you can practice the necessary skills:
  - For example, if you'll be taking an *essay* test, sometimes instructors will give you preparation essay questions to do at home, and will then select one or two for you to write about in class. If you don't get practice essays from your instructor, look for some in your textbook and practice writing the answers. Make up your own essays based on what material will be covered on the test, and then try answering them. On the day of the test, if you're given more than one essay to write, read all of the questions first before starting to answer any of them. Boyd (1988) says that reading all of the questions before starting to write your answers may help refresh your memory, and may help you choose which questions to answer if you have a choice. He also says that the questions themselves often have valuable information that may be helpful when you write your answer. Start with the question you know the best. Manage your time so that you're able to finish writing the whole test. Boyd (1988) also suggests underlining key verbs in each question since essay questions usually focus on one or more key verbs. Some key words that often appear in essay questions include: compare, which means to examine similarities and differences; summarize, which means to give the main points; discuss, which means to analyze in detail; and relate, which means to emphasize connections and associations. Boyd says that these key words will give you hints about the type of information the teacher is requesting. He also suggests making a brief outline before you start writing, since good organization is an important trait for a successful essay. Make sure you answer the questions thoroughly. Be neat, use standard English grammar, and proofread what you've written.

- If you'll be taking a *multiple-choice* exam, practice multiple-choice questions beforehand. During the test, make sure you read each entire question before selecting an answer. Read all of the alternatives as well. Look for clues in each question so that you're better able to recognize the correct alternative. Note that some words, such as *all, none, always,* and *never* indicate that the statement is an absolute without exception, so be careful when you see those words. Unless there's a penalty for an incorrect answer, take a guess on a multiple-choice test rather than leaving a question blank. You have a 20 percent to 25 percent chance of being correct by chance alone, depending on whether there are five or four alternatives. Pace yourself so that you finish the test on time. Go through the test the first time answering all the questions you know for certain. Leave the ones you're unsure of for your second time through the test. Review your work before turning in your exam. Check your answers carefully to make sure you've answered all of the questions. Make sure you've put your marks in the correct spaces if the test is machine-graded, and check to be sure you haven't made any careless mistakes.

- If you're preparing for a *short-answer* or *matching* test, practice those skills by creating short-answer and matching questions from your textbook information and class notes.

Adapted from Carr (undated); Boyd (1988);
Office of the Dean for Academic Affairs
and the Office of the Dean for Student Services,
Mercer County Community College (1996-1998).

## CHAPTER TWO

# A POSITIVE START:
## First-day Classroom Activities and Icebreakers

## The Beginning

The first class meeting of the semester is the most important one of the term! It sets the tone for the entire course — for better or worse. The first few weeks of the course, meanwhile, are crucial in helping students connect to the course, motivate themselves to learn, and discover how to persevere.

Starting the semester with *icebreakers* and other activities to get students comfortable in the classroom is becoming more widely accepted, as the research piles up showing the importance of helping students bond with their classmates so that they stay in school and graduate. One of the most significant factors that will determine whether students will persist at an institution is whether or not they feel a sense of "belonging" and "community" (Frost 1999; Tinto 1998; Wagener and Nettles 1998). How does a sense of belonging or community develop — particularly at commuter institutions? If it's going to happen at all, it will most likely happen in the classroom. Clubs and activities help students bond with the institution and with each other. But many students will merely come to campus to attend their classes, and then leave.

If you look back to your own college days, the first day of class was the day you were probably most intimidated. The instructor gave you the course syllabus, told you what was expected of you, warned you of the difficulty of the course, and, in many cases, encouraged you to withdraw from the course if you had any doubts about your level of commitment. Did this approach help you or hurt you? Did it motivate you to learn? Did it increase your commitment to the course? Whether this approach had value or not is a moot question. The fact is, it's an approach that is no longer viable and doesn't work with today's students! What does seem to work quite well for today's students is to use the first class of the semester as an opportunity for them to learn about one another. Icebreaker techniques encourage student interaction and will influence the quality and extent of future class discussions.

Today's students are different in so many ways from the students of a few decades ago. Peter Sacks (1996), a journalist and, for a short time, a college faculty member, suggests that the differences we see in today's students and in their behavior are rooted in a variety of factors. One factor is the attitude of "consumerism" among students: They tend to see themselves as "customers." Many of them believe that, because they're paying money for a degree, they're running the show. Indeed, as Howe and Strauss (2000) note in their recent book, *Millennials Rising*, one "distinguishing trait" among members of the new "Millennial Generation" or "Generation Y" — which consists of youths and young adults born after 1982, according to the authors' definition — is their high level of confidence, which some see as bordering on a sense of entitlement.

Additionally, the demographics of the United States are changing such that we have much greater diversity in our classes than we did decades ago. We are seeing an increasing number of nontraditional students, students from foreign countries, and students from an increasing variety of ethnic backgrounds. And, according to a recent report from the Educational Testing Service (Wilgoren 2000), college enrollment will expand by two million students in the next fifteen years or so. This swell in enrollment will arise from the upsurge in births in the U.S., increased immigration, and a growing belief that a college degree is an absolute necessity for a good job with a decent salary.

The ETS study suggests that 80 percent of the projected growth will be due to the expanded enrollment of minority students. Analyzing the twenty-year span from 1995 to the projections for 2015, the study finds that the presence of white students on campus will decrease from 71 percent to 63 percent. Meanwhile, African Americans' presence on campus will remain stable at 13 percent, the number of Asian Americans will increase from 5 percent to 8 percent, and the number of Hispanic Americans will rise from 11 percent to 15 percent. (Although minority college student enrollment is mushrooming, the statistics are deceiving in the sense that the numbers of Hispanic Americans and African Americans in college will not reflect the overall populations of eighteen- to twenty-four-year-olds within these groups.)

College retention rates for many groups of minority students, particularly Hispanic Americans, lag far behind those of white students. Our colleges and universities, and we as faculty in particular, must make special efforts to bring minorities into the fold of higher education, and to increase the likelihood of their success in college. One approach to encourage persistence among all students is to create an inclusive atmosphere where students from diverse backgrounds feel safe within the classroom atmosphere. For that reason, many of the icebreakers I describe here are also effective as diversity education tools. You'll also notice that many of the exercises involve students' names. Learning students' names, and having students learn each other's names, creates a classroom environment that is hospitable to learning and dialogue. Your use of students' names also helps students meet and interact with each other more easily (Wolcowitz 1984).

Let's take a look at some suggestions for getting the semester off to a great start in your classroom(s).

## Family name exercise

To help students get to know each other better, to help them (and you!) remember each other's names, and to create a sense of community in the very first class, give the Family Name Exercise a try.

*Directions:* Talk about the importance of our names for understanding our identities. When we learn how we were named — that is, who made the decision for our name and how that decision was made — we actually learn a lot about our histories. (Note: If there are students who don't have a clue as to how they were named, you can easily broaden the exercise to include them by asking some questions about their names other than how their names were selected.) I usually ask students to sit back and listen to some questions that I pose:

- Who named you?
- How was the decision for your name made?
- Are you named after someone?
- Do you know, or know of, the person who is your namesake?
- Do you like your name?
- Do some people in your life call you by a different name?
- Have you ever gone by a different name?
- Do you have a nickname?

After posing these questions, I ask the students to connect to whatever questions are most meaningful for them and to create a story about their name. I then ask them to introduce themselves to their neighbor and to share their stories with each other. This helps them meet another student and loosens them up for the large-group sharing that follows.

Before asking students to introduce themselves to the class, I get the ball rolling by sharing my entire name and telling my own story. The students then do the same.

The Family Name Exercise — which I first learned when I participated in a family therapy clinical training program — offers a remarkable memory strategy, since we all must use association to remember each other's names. The activity usually takes about 40 minutes.

## "What's in a name?" exercise

Penfield (1998) suggests that names are both personal and cultural. She says that our stories about our names are not only autobiographical, but also cross-cultural.

The "What's in a Name?" Exercise is a useful tool to help students recognize and appreciate their similarities and differences while learning each other's names.

*Directions:* Have students pair up with someone they don't know. Ask the students to interview their partners to find out the personal and cultural reasons for their first and middle names. Tell them they'll be responsible for introducing their partner to the whole class when the large group reconvenes.

Allow a few minutes for each member of the dyad to conduct the interview. When you reconvene, ask the students to introduce their partners to the class, sharing any interesting information they've gathered about their partners' names.

Write down each person's name on the blackboard or on newsprint, along with a symbol or note of something personally or culturally interesting about the person's name. After everyone has had a turn, ask the students if they've learned anything about cultural patterns in naming people, and process this information with the whole class.

Penfield (1998) suggests that, for a class of thirty, the "What's in a Name?" Exercise may take about an hour — fifteen minutes for students to work in pairs and forty-five minutes for the large-group process. You may be able to conduct the exercise in a slightly shorter amount of time, since students may need only a few minutes to conduct their partner interviews and the large-group process may not take as long as Penfield suggests.

## Stand up-sit down exercise

The Stand Up-Sit Down Exercise (Penfield 1998, citing Rutgers University 1989) is essentially a diversity-training icebreaker. The assumption behind the activity is that when you bring any group of people together, there will be both similarities and differences in their backgrounds and in other information about them. The Stand Up-Sit Down Exercise can help participants see those similarities and differences so that they can begin to appreciate them. Participants start to realize what they share with other students and how they differ.

*Directions:* Seat your students in a way that lets them see each other — a closed circle usually works best. The instructions and the actual activity take six or seven minutes for a group of any size. After the activity, allow an additional fifteen minutes to process and debrief.

Give the following directions and then read one category at a time, allowing time for students to stand up and sit down. (Note: You participate in the activity as well.) Here are the instructions as they appear in Penfield's (1998, 51) book:

> The purpose of this activity is to identify what we share and how we differ societally and in other ways through this activity. When I read a category with which you identify even partially and feel comfortable sharing with the group, please stand up and then sit down. Some of the categories are light and may seem humorous but others are more serious. Please treat the entire activity seriously. Our task is to recognize what we share with others in the group, but also to recognize those voices which are absent or outnumbered in our group.
>
> One more thing: Since this is a self-identification activity, each person will determine his or her

own identification. None of us should determine this for another. If someone does not stand, it may mean that they do not identify with the category or they do not feel comfortable sharing this identification in this group. Please do not laugh or pressure anyone into standing. OK. Please stand up and sit down if you identify with and feel comfortable with sharing the following categories.

Penfield (1998, 51-52) uses the following list of categories:

- love chocolate
- brown-eyed
- have a close family member who is, or you yourself are Jewish
- divorced
- over 30 years of age
- a man
- blue- or green-eyed
- a person of color
- have a close family member who is, or you yourself are, American Indian
- a parent
- a woman
- have a close family member who is, or you yourself are, Arab American
- vegetarian
- married or living with a partner
- care for an elderly or sick parent
- fluent in a language other than English
- have a close family member who is, or you yourself are, lesbian or gay
- left-handed
- have a twin
- have a close family member who is, or you yourself are, Hispanic American
- agnostic or atheist
- raised poor or working-class

- raised Roman Catholic
- have a close family member who is, or you yourself are, of European descent
- under 30 years of age
- have a close family member who is, or you yourself are, African American
- have a close family member who is, or you yourself are, Asian American
- raised in a Christian denomination
- have a disability, or have a close family member who has a disability
- Muslim
- born in a country other than the United States

Please offer anything I haven't mentioned that is important to your identification.

Obviously you can tailor these categories or create your own for your own classes according to what you believe is most appropriate and comfortable for your group.

Penfield does a good job of explaining the debriefing process that follows the activity. First, she says students will have reactions to the activity itself. Did the students expect certain categories that were excluded? Were they surprised by the categories that were included?

Another discussion that usually follows the exercise involves the recognition of how any one of these categories, by itself, limits our understanding of our whole identities and the identities of others. Through this activity, your students have an opportunity to look at the assumptions they make about people in certain categories. You can ask students if they have any observations and learnings they'd like to share with the whole group. Penfield says she also asks participants to notice if there were categories for which there were no student representatives. She points out that, if certain groups aren't "spoken for" in the class, their perspectives will be missing from future discussions.

"What's in a Name?" and Stand Up-Sit Down are just two of many wonderful diversity training exercises you can find in Penfield's (1998) *Respecting Diversity, Working for Equity: A Handbook for Trainers*.

I should mention that the Stand-Up-Sit Down Exercise also works without a formal diversity perspective. Some instructors use it solely as a fun and light icebreaker, with lifestyle categories like these:

- Eat pizza more than once a week.
- Go to the movies at least twice a month.
- Drive more than 30 minutes to get to school.
- Listen to the "oldies" station(s) on the radio.

## Activities that help students find commonalities

The following exercises are all aimed at promoting bonding by helping students find things they share in common.

*Directions:* Ask students to raise their hands in response to a number of questions like these:

- How many of you have moved three or more times in your lifetime?
- How many of you have three or more siblings?
- How many of you were born in another country?
- How many of you have traveled outside the United States?

Let your imagination be your guide as to the questions you ask.

After each question, pair up students who have raised their hands. Once the whole class is in pairs, tell the students that they've each found a classmate with whom they have at least one thing in common. Tell them they'll have two minutes to talk to find out how many other experiences or traits they share.

*Directions:* Ask students to raise their hands in response to questions like the last four questions in the Stand Up-Sit Down Exercise above. Add some academically oriented questions, such as, "How many of you plan to major in history?" or, "How many of you are planning a career in teaching?" After students have raised their hands in response to five or six questions and observed their classmates' responses, have them form four-person groups that you select either randomly or by some design. (Some instructors move students around in what appears to be a random fashion, but they're actually creating groups that are gender and culturally diverse.)

Next, hand out newsprint and magic markers to each group. Tell the students in each group to find four things they share in common, and to depict these commonalties any way they choose: They can draw pictures, use symbols, or, as a last resort, use words. Encourage the students to be as creative as possible. Tell them that each member of the group will introduce himself or herself later to the class, and will describe one of the four things he or she shares in common with the other students in his or her group. (Instead of having the group select a "spokesperson," asking students to each speak for themselves is a way to get all of them speaking on the first day of class.)

After 10 minutes of group work, reconvene the class.

Within the small groups, the students usually have fun and some bonding occurs. But the students are also interested in learning what the other groups have to say. This activity allows for both; it's a great way to set a comfortable, sharing tone for the rest of the semester.

*Directions* (adapted from Berko and Aitken et al. 1998): Ask the students to arrange themselves along an imaginary line, either along a side wall or down the middle of the room. Tell the students they need to arrange themselves in single-file along this line according to questions that you're about to give them. Some sample questions:

- How many brothers and sisters do you have?
- If you could be any animal, what would it be?
- How athletic are you?
- How creative are you?
- Do you play a musical instrument? If so, which one?

For some questions, you can show the students what the front of the line represents and what the end of the line means. For example, for the first question about brothers and sisters, you could say that the front of the line is for only children and the back of the line is for "the birth of a nation" (as Berko and Aitken call it).

After the students have arranged themselves along the line — a process that will take quite a bit of negotiation and interaction! Ask them to count off by twos. Have each Number 1 stand on the right side of the line facing the

Number 2 behind him or her. Ask each pair to exchange names; then, the Number 1's can share anything about the topic they'd like with their partners, for one or two minutes. The Number 2's can then talk about the same topic with the same partner for the same amount of time.

After each question, the students rearrange themselves in the line according to their responses to the next question. You can use many questions so that the students will get a chance to meet several people in the class. Just be sure the students are meeting different students with each pairing.

*Directions:* Have your students fill out the Personal Reference Inventory (PRI) on the first day of class. (You'll find the PRI at the end of this chapter. You could also develop your own questions tailored to your own classes.)

After students complete the inventory, have them pair off by numbering themselves as "1" or "2" and asking the 1's to join the 2's. Then, ask them to discuss their responses to the questions with each other. (Note: I always tell my students that it's completely up to them to decide what to share with each other and at what level or depth.) For each pairing, both students can respond to the same question, starting at the top of the list.

After a two-minute period, interrupt the proceedings and ask the 1's to pair up with new 2's to share with each other on the next topic.

## Introduction by identities exercise

Another excellent icebreaker that promotes diversity is the Introduction by Identities Exercise.

One of my colleagues teaches an English class to international students. She begins her first day by asking the students to tell a little about themselves. She starts the exercise by role modeling examples of what the students might share. (Again, in all of these activities, you need to make it clear to students that they can decide what to share about themselves and at what depth.) My colleague tells the students her name, with a related anecdote about how she was named. She says that, obviously, she is female, that she is Italian American, that she was raised Catholic, and that she was born in the United States.

Within her extremely diverse class, the students then start to share something about themselves, and some early bonding begins to take place.

## Student disclosure exercises

In order to encourage interaction among your students, consider these ice-breakers or variations on them:

*Directions:* Give a 3x5 index card to each student. Have the students write their names on one side of the card and, on the other side, something distinctive or special about themselves that they would not mind others in the class knowing. Then, ask the students to circulate, introducing themselves to each other and sharing what they've written about themselves. You can participate in the circulation as well.

Next, collect the cards and read the backs of them aloud. You can then either ask the students to introduce themselves as their cards are read, or ask the student who met the person whose card is read to introduce that student to the class.

As a variation on this activity, once the student circulation around the room ends, have the students introduce themselves to the class and describe something distinctive about themselves. Each student must say his or her own name, then the names of the previous student(s), and then repeat his or her own name and share something unique about himself or herself. This variation uses the mnemonic devices of association and repetition to help students learn each other's names.

*Directions:* Put three or four questions on the blackboard or on an overhead transparency. Here are some examples of questions you could use:

- If you were invisible, what would you do for a day?
- What is the most frightening thing that's ever happened to you?
- If your house was burning down, what item(s) would you save and why?
- Who has been the most positive influence in your life?
- If you could travel anywhere in the world, where would it be and why?

Ask the students to respond in writing to whatever question they choose. Then, have students pair up, introduce themselves to each other, and share a response to any of the questions. After a couple of minutes, ask the students to introduce themselves to the class, sharing their names and any information concerning their responses to the questions. (As in all self-disclosure exercises, remind students that it is always their choice as to what to share and at what depth.)

## Dyadic interviews.

Dyadic interviews are designed to help students get to know each other well enough to introduce each other to the rest of the class.

*Directions:* Ask students to jot down three questions they wouldn't mind being asked about themselves. Explain that the questions can be at any level of self-disclosure they choose, and that their responses may become public information for the class (so they shouldn't reveal any information they want to be private). You can let students select their own partners — in which case they usually pair up with students sitting next to them — or you can pair up students in what appears to be a random fashion, but that really reflects pairs of diverse students according to gender, race/ethnicity, or age.

Tell the students to switch papers with their partners so that the students have their partners' questions to ask. The students can then conduct short interviews and jot down their partners' responses on their sheets. (Be sure to remind the students to get their partners' full names and correct pronunciations.)

You serve as timekeeper for the activity. If you have an uneven number of students in your class, you can either participate in the activity yourself or ask one dyad to work as a triad.

After a few minutes, interrupt the students so that the interviewers and interviewees can switch roles.

Once all of the students have had the opportunity to interview and to be interviewed, reconvene the large group and ask each student to introduce his or her partner to the class. Be sure the students introduce their partners by using their full names, and that they share with the class any information they've learned from their interviews. Their partners may add to or clarify anything that is shared.

### Dyadic sharing using drawing or writing.

*Directions:* Ask each of your students to draw or write three things that help describe who they are. Then, put the students in pairs and have them share what they've produced with each other. You can then ask the students to introduce themselves and explain to the class what they've drawn or written, or have the students introduce their partners and explain their partners' productions.

Informal sharing exercise. In an informal sharing exercise, students pair up, introduce themselves to each other, and share any information about themselves that isn't obvious to others. You can use this activity as a warm-up for students to introduce themselves to the class, or ask the students to introduce their partners to the class.

You'll want to be sure to participate in this exercise in some way. You can pair up with a student if there are an uneven number of students in the class, or you can simply introduce yourself to the class when the students are finished with the large-group process. You might also invite students to ask questions about you or the course.

### "Walk around the room" exercise.

The "Walk around the Room" exercise can take many forms. Students can simply walk around the room and meet as many other people as possible within some limited time frame.

*Directions:* You can ask the students to share just their names, or you can create a theme that students can talk about in addition to sharing their names. The theme can relate to your particular course. For example, in a social psychology course in which one of the topics we cover is friendship formation, I sometimes have students share their names and the qualities they most value in a close friendship. In a math course, you might ask students to share their names and their first experience with math in grade school.

Try to select something straightforward so that all of the students will have something to say. Silberman (1996) suggests an exercise he calls "Trading Places." For it, you give students "sticky" notes on which they write something either about themselves or about their opinions and their thinking. The students then walk around the room, introducing themselves to a number of other students and trading notes with other students who possess some idea, opinion, or experience they'd like to acquire. The trades have to be mutual, and students may trade as many times as they like.

When you reconvene the whole class, have the students share the trades they made and their reasons for doing so.

## Scavenger hunt.

*Directions:* Ask students to circulate around the room looking for people who fit certain categories. For example:

- Someone who is an only child.
- Someone who has lived abroad.
- Someone who speaks more than one language.
- Someone who has many siblings.
- Someone who has the same major or program of study as you.

You can also include statements that revolve around class content or personal background information.

Tell the students that when they meet someone who matches a category, they should write down the person's name. Encourage the students to meet different people, even if the same person might fit more than one category.

When you reconvene the whole class, process the exercise by asking the students to introduce the people they've met and share what they've learned about them.

(Note: This exercise is an adaptation of one suggested by Silberman [1996].)

## "Wheel within a wheel."

"Wheel within a Wheel" is an exercise designed to help students meet several other classmates, as well as to build self-esteem and create energy in the classroom. The exercise is also known as the "Circle-to-Circle" icebreaker, and is described in detail by Joesting (1978).

*Directions:* Ask half of your students to sit in a circle in the center of the room, facing outward. Next, have the rest of the students form an outer circle, facing the other students. With an even number of students everyone will have a partner.

The inner group remains seated throughout the exercise; the outer circle rotates to the right, one person at a time, for each part of the activity. (Note: If you have a small class, you may want to have the students in the outer circle rotate until they reach their original partner. Otherwise, you may ask them to rotate only until they've met several other students.)

With each new pairing, ask the students to discuss a new topic you suggest. Select topics that will get the students thinking about and sharing things that will raise their self-esteem. Give each pairing about two minutes to share with each other. Then, ask the students to rotate and introduce themselves to the next person.

Some topics that are self-esteem boosters:

- What do you consider to be one of your biggest accomplishments in life?
- What person have you affected in a positive way? How?
- What goal have you achieved that you found particularly difficult?
- What person has most affected your life in a positive way? How?
- What do you consider to be your most positive personality traits?

If circles are too cumbersome for your classroom, you can do the same exercise by simply asking students to pair up with a different partner for each topic. (Note: This exercise is adapted from Joesting [1978].)

*Alphabetize exercise.*

*Directions:* Have the students alphabetize themselves, by first name, along one wall of the classroom. In order to do this, the students must interact with each other. You can then have each student introduce himself or herself to the class.

For variety, you might ask the students to name one, two, or three other students so that all of you can learn by repetition.

*Introductions and repetition.*

*Directions:* In this activity, students volunteer to introduce themselves to the class and share something about themselves that might help the other students remember them. (Note: It usually works better to have students volunteer rather than to go around the room in seating order, because students may "wait their turn" with anxiety and tune out other students' names and stories.)

Encourage the students to listen carefully to each other's names, and tell them they'll have to name three other people at the end of the exercise.

After all of the students have introduced themselves, have each student introduce three other students to the class, stating each student's name and what the student has revealed about himself or herself. The students can choose any three people they'd like, but they can't name students who have already been introduced. The repetition helps everyone remember each other's names — though, at the end, you'll run out of people for the last several students to introduce. Even so, the exercise still energizes the students as they leave the room.

## Introducing yourself

To show your students that you're a human being, you might want to share some things about yourself. For example, you can talk about the story of your interest in your discipline or your interest in the particular course you're teaching. You might tell the students about when you studied the same course, what you expected, what you worried about, how you studied, any great wisdom you gained, or any other anecdotal information they might find interesting or helpful in some way. In many surveys, students say they appreciate teachers who are approachable. By disclosing some information about your interests, hobbies, and leisure activities, your students will — from the very first class — see you as more than just their instructor.

You can achieve a similar objective by having your students ask you their own questions about you. Have the students write their questions on index cards. You can then read and respond to them in class (thus giving yourself the chance to screen the questions as well).

You might also simply ask your students if they have any questions they'd like to ask you about yourself. You could joke with them and say, "You can ask me anything at all. Of course, I may choose not to answer, depending on what you ask." I've found that students often ask pretty mundane questions, such as "Are you married?" "Do you have children?" and "What are your interests and hobbies apart from teaching?" Occasionally, though, they'll ask more thoughtful questions, such as "If you could do something else with your life apart from teaching, what would it be?" or "Why did you choose college teaching?" You can even have students work in groups of four to develop questions that a group reporter will ask for the group.

## Course expectation activities

*Directions:* Write the name of your course on the blackboard. Ask the students to write down three expectations or questions they have about the course. Then, put the students in four-person groups and tell them they must reach consensus about their expectations. Have each group pick a recorder who will take notes and report to the whole class what the group has agreed upon.

After all of the groups have reported, discuss the students' expectations and describe what the course is (really) all about.

*Directions:* Give each student a 3x5 index card and ask them to write down any questions they have pertaining to the course they're about to start. Then, collect the cards and read the questions aloud, commenting on them in terms of when and how the course might address them.

To make the exercise more interactive, ask the students to share their questions first in four-person groups or dyads.

*Directions:* Many instructors hand out the syllabus on the first day, go over it briefly, and ask students if they have any questions. This is often followed by silence. Robert Magnan (1990) suggests a variation that gets students more engaged with the course and with you. He recommends handing out the syllabus and then giving students some time to read it privately. You can then divide the students into four-person groups. Tell them to decide together on questions to ask about the course and about you. Encourage them to ask questions about any aspect of the class or about you, whether professional or personal.

Have each group select a spokesperson who will ask the questions for the group when the whole class reconvenes. Magnan says that many of the questions will be about the obvious — grading, expectations, assignments, and attendance. There may also be more questions than usual, as students are more likely to ask questions when they feel they're speaking for others as well as themselves.

Magnan found questions about the instructor to be similar to those I mentioned above: Students typically wonder about your credentials for teaching the course, your experiences outside of teaching, what you like or dislike about the course or about teaching in general, why you became a college teacher, what your other interests are, and whether you're married and if you have children.

## Your Goal:
## A Relaxed Atmosphere from Day 1

Find icebreakers and activities you're comfortable with. The goal is to start the semester by developing a relaxed learning atmosphere. Students want the classroom to be safe and friendly. Since meeting other students is fun, your students will begin to develop a positive attitude about your course, and get an initial sense that your classroom is a "welcoming" one — an important attribute that we cover in depth in Chapter 3.

# Personal Reference Inventory (PRI)

- Name
- Who is your hero?
- Define a "politician."
- What irritates you the most about this world? Why?
- What do you consider to be your greatest accomplishment? Why?
- If you won $1 million in the lottery, how would you spend the money?
- What celebrity would you like to change places with? Why?
- What would be the title of a book about your life story? Why?
- Describe your most embarrassing circumstance.
- What would you like to change about your past? Why?
- How would you respond if you discovered that your best same-sex friend was homosexual?
- Discuss your impressions of "wealthy" people.
- Which three adjectives best describe your relational abilities (i.e., your abilities to get along with others)?
- Which part of the world would you like to visit? Why?
- Which food best describes your personality? Why?
- What is the most important discovery in life? Why?
- Who is/was your greatest influence? Why?
- What does "sexism" mean to you?
- What does a grade of "A" mean to you?
- Do you believe in reincarnation? Why?

From Berko, et al.,
*Handbook of Instructional Options with Test Items.*
7th edition. Copyright © 1998 by Houghton Mifflin Company.
Used with permission.

CHAPTER THREE

# CREATING A WELCOMING
# CLASSROOM ENVIRONMENT

> ...[T]he emotional climate of the classroom is directly
> related to the attainment of academic excellence,
> however defined. Students' feelings about what they
> experience in class — whether inclusion or exclusion,
> mastery or inadequacy, support or hostility — cannot be
> divorced from what and how well they learn.
> — Wilkinson and Ansell 1992, 4

## Creating the Environment

Ask any student or professor what the most important factors are for student success in college and you'll likely hear: student preparedness, student ability and motivation, attendance, and teacher effectiveness. I have put this question to both my students and my colleagues, and these responses have been the most frequent answers I've encountered. I was surprised, therefore, to discover in the college student retention literature that one of the most important factors in whether students persist to earn a degree is whether or not they experience a sense of *belonging* at their institutions.

By now the evidence is irrefutable that student success has an affective dimension — that is, it is tied to how students *feel* in class and at the institution. Retention studies conducted over the last two decades in higher education suggest that one of the most crucial factors in helping students complete their studies is creating an atmosphere of *community* (see Bank, Biddle, and Slavings 1990; Frost 1999; Padilla 1999). Do students feel they belong at a particular institution? Do students have friends at the institution? The bottom line for retention seems to have more to do with students' friendships than with their studies. So how can we as faculty promote that sense of belonging in our classes? In this chapter we'll look at strategies you can use to connect with your students and promote student-student interaction.

As I pointed out in Chapter 2, retention rates for many groups of minority college students — particularly for Hispanic Americans — lag far behind those of more traditional (i.e., white) students. Those of us who teach at colleges and universities — particularly commuter institutions — and who are committed to increasing those retention rates recognize that if student friendships are to occur at all, they'll probably occur within the classroom. This makes classroom atmosphere and dynamics critical variables for retention. The challenge to us as faculty goes beyond learning to teach effectively, and beyond using multifaceted approaches and strategies. Equally important — in terms of fostering student persistence — is to create an inclusive atmosphere where students from diverse backgrounds feel safe within the classroom environment. Students need to believe that their voices will be heard and valued by their teachers and their peers. Within such a climate, the chances that students will form friendships go up markedly.

If we want to motivate students to learn our course content and persist to earn a degree, we need to pay attention to more than how we can best present course material. We also need to manage the class dynamics in such a way as to foster bonding among students. Effective teachers create an atmosphere of trust and warmth between themselves and their students — and they cultivate that same atmosphere among the students themselves.

## The "Chilly Classroom Climate"

The "chilly classroom climate" research of the last two decades documents differential treatment of students in classes ranging from grade school through graduate school. This information has been extensively discussed in feminist journals, at women's conferences, and in multicultural journals and conferences. Yet the research has not become a part of general educational discourse.

### Observations

Hall and Sandler (1982) wrote the first comprehensive report on differential treatment of men and women in the college classroom. The term "chilly climate" was coined to describe the classroom atmosphere for many women in colleges and universities. Hall and Sandler found in their research myriad gender inequities, some of them small and, at first glance, trivial, and some that were quite profound. Even the small inequities, when taken together, created an environment for women that was inhospitable at the least and hostile at the worst.

The term *micro-inequities* was coined by Rowe (1977) to describe the many small and subtle ways people are treated differently in the classroom because of their gender, race/ethnicity, sexual orientation, or age. While most of the related research has been conducted on differential treatment of women, these other groups of students have been considered "outsider" groups in academia as well.

Grade-school-classroom studies, many of them using videotapes of teacher behavior, have clearly demonstrated that teachers generally pay more attention to boys than girls, in numerous ways. Teachers ask boys harder questions, allow them more time to answer questions, ask more probing follow-up questions, and give boys more praise and criticism than they give girls (Sadker and Sadker 1994). In addition, other research shows that grade school teachers tend to give boys specific instructions on how to complete a project or task. In contrast, teachers more often show girls how to do a project or even do it for them (Sandler and Hoffman 1992).

Hall and Sandler's (1982) review of research for all educational levels shows six major ways in which teachers communicate sex-role expectations to students:

- Teachers call on male students more often than on female students.
- Teachers coach males to work for a fuller answer more often than they coach females to do so.
- Teachers wait longer for males to answer questions than they wait for females before going on to another student.
- Teachers are more likely to ask female students questions that require factual answers.
- Teachers respond more extensively to male students' comments than to female students' comments.
- Teachers communicate sex-role stereotypes by their use of sexist language.

Myra and David Sadker, university professors who have studied teacher-student interactions in grade school classrooms, have shown (1994) that many teachers are not conscious of their contributions toward gender inequities in the classroom. Teachers who believed they were being "fair" were often shocked to see themselves on videotape behaving in differential ways that were completely hidden to them. This finding has led us to understand that what happens in the classroom may be overt and obvious, or it may be much more subtle and elusive. The challenges we face in our classes may, therefore, involve some soul-searching and consciousness-raising.

According to a study done by the American Association of University Women (cited in Sadker and Sadker 1994), one result of differential treatment of grade school girls is that, during high school, girls' self-esteem levels tend to drop relative to those of boys. Further, the same study showed that girls have lower career aspirations than boys even when their potential and their successes are comparable.

While some studies report gender differences in self-esteem (e.g., Kelly and Jordon 1990, Widaman et al. 1992), other studies do not find overall gender differences in self-esteem (e.g., Côté 1996, Cate and Sugawara 1986). One consistent finding, reported by Matlin (2000), is that both adolescent boys and girls who score high in "masculinity" have higher self-esteem. In particular, those adolescents who score high on the "instrumentality" dimension of masculinity — that is, the ones who believe they can accomplish goals — have higher self-esteem (Cate and Sugawara 1986, Rose and Montemayor 1994, Stein et al. 1992, Worell 1989). The burning question then becomes, To what extent do our schools foster or discourage instrumentality in females and in other "outsider" groups of students?

Sandler and Hoffman (1992) suggest that the types of grade-school-classroom practices described above, combined with sexism in society at large, contribute to a classroom atmosphere in which women's contributions and women's words seem less valuable to us. In a classic study done by Goldberg (1968), female college students gave higher grades to essays they thought were written by males. Identical essays allegedly written by women were judged as inferior. This study, along with so many others, shows us that women incorporate the same societal messages of female inferiority as do men. Study after study, in all fields and disciplines, documents similar findings. Although a meta-analysis of the research, done by Janet Swim and her colleagues (1989), did not support overall prejudice against women and their work, newer studies of the 1990s (e.g., Haslett et al. 1992, Eagly et al. 1992, Eagly and Mladinic 1994, Fiske 1993) show that bias against women is alive and well under certain conditions. Bias has been documented when a woman's competence is being judged in a traditionally masculine area, or when a woman is acting in a stereotypically masculine way. Bias has also been found where there is little information available about the qualifications of the woman being judged, and when males are doing the evaluating.

Studies have shown that, in North American culture, gender may be the most salient characteristic we notice when we first encounter someone (Bem 1993, Unger 1988). It seems to be even more salient than race, ethnicity, or age. We all develop gender *schemas* very early in life. We categorize people as males or females, and then gender schemas shape our perceptions, thoughts, expectations, and behaviors of ourselves and others. This happens both consciously and unconsciously, and it occurs in all aspects of our lives.

The classroom is no exception. Faculty and students come to the college classroom with a host of gender-related expectations. Most faculty members would probably like to believe that they don't hold stereotypes, expectations, prejudices, or biases of any type. However, none of us can escape the socialization process that has shaped our understandings of our social worlds. At this point, there is extensive empirical and anecdotal evidence that many faculty members, both men and women, treat women and men differently in the classroom. These behaviors may be overt — as, for example, by the use of language, statements, or questions that are in some way gender biased — or they may be more subtle, such as nonverbal cues, gestures, and eye contact. In either case, the behaviors may be conscious or completely outside the instructor's awareness.

The Sadkers' (1994) research documented a lack of awareness on the part of faculty in their patterns of behavior in the classroom. An experimental group of twenty-three instructors who had participated in a gender awareness workshop, along with a control group of twenty-three instructors who had not participated, viewed a videotape on classroom behavior. The first time the experimental subjects viewed the videotape, they believed the instructor was treating all of the students similarly. In their second viewing, however — which followed the gender awareness workshop — the subjects realized that the instructor in the videotape had asked three times as many questions of the male students and given four times as much praise to male students in comparison to female students. Additionally, when the experimental subjects were compared to the control subjects who had not attended the gender awareness workshop, there were significant differences in the classroom behaviors among members of the two groups. Instructors who had participated in the gender awareness workshop conducted classes that were more interactive; male and female students participated equally and there was more student participation in general. Moreover, these instructors gave more precise feedback on students' comments and questions and demonstrated less gender bias in their teaching in comparison to the control group instructors (Sadker and Sadker 1990).

C.G. Krupnick (1985) conducted a study at Wheaton College in Massachusetts two years after the formerly all-women institution admitted men for the first time. The study showed that, although only 10 percent of the students in class were men, the male students did 25 percent of the speaking in class. This pattern occurred even though the classes were predominantly female and the majority of faculty members were also female. Analysis of videotapes of classroom sessions at this same institution further showed that men put their hands up to answer questions faster than women did, and that women were more likely to expand the previous speaker's ideas rather than challenge them (Fiske 1990). I discovered a similar pattern of male domination of the discussion in my "Psychology of Women" course, which also had a majority of women (see McGlynn 2000/September 8 and McGlynn 2000/September 22).

In 1996, Sandler, Silverberg, and Hall summarized the research from the 1980s and 1990s in a book called *The Chilly Classroom Climate: A Guide to Improve the Education of Women*. While the Hall and Sandler work published in 1982 focused specifically on the teacher behaviors that contribute to a chilly climate, this more recent work goes beyond teacher behavior and examines how the classroom atmosphere is impacted by classroom structure, power dynamics, teaching styles, the curriculum, and the relationships among students.

## Implications

In *The Chilly Classroom Climate*, the authors make several assumptions that seem relevant for our understanding of classroom atmosphere. The authors presume that learning is facilitated when students are active contributors and teachers are responsive to them. Students may be active learners in a number of ways. They may participate by practicing active listening skills, taking notes, working in pairs or larger groups, or asking questions and making comments.

Sandler et al. (1996) further believe that teacher-student interactions affect not only the level of student participation, but also students' learning, self-esteem, satisfaction, and even their motivation to succeed and their career choices. In their research, the authors cite evidence that both male and female faculty members treat students differently based on gender, and that they often do so completely unknowingly. The authors suggest that the subtle ways faculty treat women differently also affect other groups — for example, students of color; students who speak with a foreign or regional accent; lesbian, gay, bisexual, and transgender students; older students; students with disabilities; and "working-class" students. These are the groups we referred to above as "outsider" groups. These other factors in addition to gender — factors such as race/ethnicity, age, sexual orientation, level of ability, and social class — are also critical variables affecting teacher-student interactions, which, in turn, affect students' classroom experiences.

Sandler et al. (1996) believe that, while all students would benefit from the recommendations for good teaching that follow from their research, good teaching alone cannot eliminate the effects of bias. This is where faculty awareness becomes important. The authors caution readers that their research necessarily involves generalizations about people — and generalizations are always subject to exceptions. Not all women or all men, all Hispanics or all Asians, etc., behave in such and such a way. The generalizations simply tell us that certain groups of people are more likely to behave in a particular way. The generalizations help us understand how gender, race/ethnicity, age, etc., tend to affect teacher-student interactions and what follows from the atmosphere created in the classroom.

A number of studies that followed the 1982 report on the "chilly classroom climate" were conducted throughout the United States. Some climate studies found very little difference in faculty behavior toward men and women and little difference in level or quality of participation among their male and female students. Heller, Puff, and Mills (1985) suggested that the "chilly climate" might be more manifest in certain institutions than in others, or in certain programs within institutions.

Other research (e.g., Constantinople et al. 1988, Cornelius et al. 1990) found that additional factors — such as class size, discipline, and time of semester — were actually more influential on student participation than was the gender of instructor or student. These studies concluded that teacher behavior does not greatly influence student participation, and therefore targeting faculty behavior for change was inappropriate. Crawford and MacLeod (1990) found that, regardless of the size of the institution, class size was the factor most important to student participation. In fact, the researchers said, class size seemed to influence students' perceptions as to whether a course encouraged participation, and whether students as individuals could participate and were free to assert their ideas.

Sandler, Silverberg, and Hall's (1996) summary and analysis of all the previous research makes several points to address the issues raised above. First, the researchers who found differences in student participation based on gender, but who did not believe those differences were related to faculty members' differential treatment of men and women, may be right. Sandler et al. agree that students may actually *bring* differences *to* the classroom. Obviously, female students have lived a life of experience that has already shaped their way of being in the world and in the classroom. Sandler et al. further agree that what perpetuates gender differences in classroom participation may not be overt discrimination of any kind on the part of the instructor. Rather, it may be the instructor's lack of attention and awareness to gender that exacerbates women's negative classroom experience, where it exists. We as faculty, then, may need to take a much more proactive stance to remedy the host of factors that might contribute to lower classroom participation by women. In other words, even in cases in which we are not the cause of women's inhibitions in the classroom, we need to be part of the solution.

## Alternatives

*The Chilly Classroom Climate* offers many recommendations to assist us as we attempt to increase student involvement in our classes. The Sandler et al. suggestions will help us develop a variety of teaching strategies to reach a diverse student population. The recommendations I'll be offering from the Sandler et al. research, from other sources, and from my own community college students are not about accommodating women and other "outsider" groups. The strategies presented throughout this book are about enhancing the learning environment for women, for students of color, for older students ... for *all* students. Crawford and MacLeod (1990) conclude that lower participation among female students, and among other students who are reticent to speak in class, is best managed by teachers who are aware of the research and who have developed a variety of teaching methodologies to create a "student-friendly" classroom.

Do some of our students, for whatever reason(s), feel excluded in our classes? The modified focus groups I conducted for several years (beginning in the late 1980s) with Mercer County Community College students, and the more recent Spring 1996 and Fall 2000 surveys I conducted concerning classroom atmosphere, generated the same kinds of comments and recommendations as has the more formal research.

Faculty-student interaction seems to play a big role in students' comfort levels in class. Many educators believe that student success is more likely if students feel safe in class. Is the classroom atmosphere conducive to students feeling they're respected, supported, and encouraged to learn by their instructors? Do they have a sense of belonging to a community? Do they feel that their instructors and their institution care about them and their futures?

The ideal classroom atmosphere is one in which students feel connected to you the instructor as well as to their classmates. There are many ways you can connect with students personally. There are also activities you can use to promote student-student connections. The general classroom atmosphere is dependent upon the quality of these relationships. And remember, the atmosphere of your class is set in place the very first day the course begins. If you can make connections with your students, and your students can bond with their classmates, early on in the semester, you will have established a "successful beginning." This start will allow rapport and trust to grow stronger and stronger, making your classroom a more effective learning environment.

## What Students Want from Us as Faculty

Certainly students' relationships with us as faculty play an important role in their sense of belonging. Perlman and McCann (1998) published the results of a study in which they asked seven hundred undergraduates to write complaints about teaching behaviors they had observed in all the courses they'd taken. Among the top ten complaints of teacher behaviors were: "being unhelpful and unapproachable" and "intellectual arrogance — talking down to or showing a lack of respect for students."

What interests me most about the Perlman and McCann results are the parallels I found in research I conducted during the Fall 2000 semester with the majority of my 220 students in "Introduction to Psychology." Although I posed two very different questions in comparison to those Perlman and McCann used, students still identified similar factors as important to them. In my research, I asked two open-ended questions:

- In all of the college and high school courses you have taken, are there teaching methods, strategies, or techniques that are particularly helpful to the way(s) you learn?
- Are there teacher behaviors — in other words, are there things that teachers say or do — that motivate you to learn and to do well?

In my research, students not only wrote their responses privately on index cards, but I also had them work in focus groups of four students per group. Within the groups, students were asked to share their responses and to reach consensus on the five most important factors they had identified. I then reconvened the focus groups into the larger class and asked each group's recorder/reporter to state their top five factors. This large-group sharing allowed for some clarification and for a rich discussion.

If we really listen to our students, the retention literature that focuses on the importance of bonding and classroom atmosphere makes perfect sense. Although they may use different language, students overwhelmingly report that classroom atmosphere is a critical variable in what motivates them to come to class and do well. In response to my second research question regarding motivational qualities of instructors, students said over and

63

over again how important it is to them to have an instructor who is approachable and who speaks to them at a level they understand. (Note the similarity with the Perlman and McCann results, despite the different angle their research took!)

In follow-up discussion with students, when I asked for specifics on what it means to be "approachable," students said things like the following:

- It's important to me that the instructor knows my name and a little bit about who I am.
- I want to feel as if the instructor cares whether I come to class, and that he or she is invested in me learning the material and doing well.
- I want the instructor to be "human." (Note: When I asked for further elaboration, students said they want their instructors to be personal — to not always be in the "teacher" role. They want us to share a little of who we are outside the teacher role.)
- I want the instructor to use humor in class.
- I want to feel as if the instructor respects me as a person, and respects my opinions.
- I want my instructor to show enthusiasm about the discipline and about teaching.

This last statement about teacher enthusiasm was the most frequently expressed comment of all. Given this fact, colleges and universities may need to rethink professional development and renewal opportunities for faculty members, particularly for those of us who have been teaching for decades. Clearly our students are telling us how to create a safe environment and giving us tips on how to build rapport with them.

## How to Build Rapport and Connect with Your Students

Now that you've learned about the importance of a welcoming classroom atmosphere in enhancing your students' participation in class, and ultimately the quality of their learning experience, you're ready to begin the hands-on practical strategies that will help you create such an atmosphere. Building rapport and connecting with your students — from Day 1 — is the first step. Here are some tips to help you do just that:

**#1: *When you walk into class the first day, and every day, greet he class as a whole or greet students individually.*** This can be as simple as smiling and saying, "Hi!" Students are reinforced when you greet them as if you're pleased to see them. It's a simple task, yet it goes very far in establishing warmth in the classroom.

**#2**: *In your first class, tell the students what you prefer to be called.* Then ask each of them what they prefer to be called. Students are often non-committal, and sometimes it takes gentle prodding to find out if they have a nickname or another name their friends call them. Once you find out each student's preference, write it down in your roll book so you remember it. If you need to make marks in your book to help you pronounce each student's name, do so. Ask students to correct you if you mispronounce their names.

Although you may be burdened by large classes, find ways to learn students' names early in the semester. Mostly, this simply takes motivation on your part. You'll likely be more motivated when you realize the difference it may make in terms of student participation and learning. In most of the research on retention and classroom climate, and from students' own reports, when you as an instructor know your students' names, the students will feel more comfortable with and positive about your class.

Wolcowitz (1984) offers some tips that will help you learn your students' names. He suggests using index cards featuring students' names and other information you can use to call roll in lieu of a class list. That way, you can easily match students' names and faces. In my "Introduction to Psychology" large-lecture class of 220 students, I ask students to bring in a recent photo. I tape the students' photos to their index cards and write down some information about each student to help me associate his/her name with his/her face. I use the cards like flash cards to help my memory. In particular, I look at the cards before I meet the students in twenty-person seminar classes so that I'll be able to remember their names.

**#3**: *In general, it works best to call all students by either their first or last names.* If given the choice, most students will elect to be called by their first name, which creates an atmosphere that is less formal and more friendly. However, if you and the students are more comfortable with last names, you can call the men "Mr." and the women "Ms." (unless they request to be addressed differently).

**#4**: *Take roll in every class session.* Boll and Parkman (1988) discuss the importance of roll taking as a way to encourage class attendance, show we value our students' presence in class, and foster student participation in class. These educators argue that students like to hear their names spoken. Calling roll helps you remember your students' names and lets the students learn each other's names as well.

Boll and Parkman suggest that you ask questions during the roll-taking process. They tell their own students, for instance, that when roll is called, they're to answer the roll by responding to a general question, posed at the beginning of the class. Early in the semester, the questions are safe and easy for everyone to answer. Examples:

- What's your program of study or major?
- Where were you born?
- What's your favorite food?

As the semester progresses, the questions ask for more self-disclosure. Examples:

- What's your favorite TV program?
- If you had to give a book as a gift, what book would you choose?
- If you could ask anyone three questions and receive an honest answer, who would you approach and what would you ask?

After the semester is in full swing, the questions can relate to course content:

- If you could gain one punctuation skill, what would it be? (a lead-in to a review of punctuation)
- What chemical reaction that occurs in your daily life do you most value? (a lead-in to a chemistry lecture)

Boll and Parkman say that after just a few classes, students begin to anticipate the questions and many students have suggestions for additional questions. Boll and Parkman note that an excellent source for questions is Gregory Stock's (1987) *The Book of Questions*.

**#5**: *Use your students' names in class in ways that will boost their self-*esteem. For example, you might quote a comment a student made earlier in the class if it's appropriate to a point you're now making. (Be sure, however, to use minority and female students' comments as frequently as you do white male students' comments, since doing the latter is one of the clearest inadvertent differential treatment practices found in the "chilly classroom climate" research.) Where appropriate, praise individuals for their questions, comments, answers to questions in class, test grades, papers they've written, and work they've submitted. At the end of a good class discussion, or when an entire class does well on a test or project, praise the class as a whole. If a particular student does poorly on a test, paper, or project, speak to him/her privately and ask if he/she knows what went wrong and how he/she might do better in the future. You can offer some guidance for improvement in a nonjudgmental way.

**#6: *Since the frequency of faculty-student contact inside and outside of class seems to promote student motivation, perseverance, and success, talk to students before and after class.*** At the very beginning of the semester, give students your office location, office hours, phone extension (with voice mail instructions), and e-mail address. Invite students to your office by telling them it's OK to drop by, by establishing conference appointments with them, and by asking them to pick up their work at your office.

**#7: *In surveys of student satisfaction with the college experience, students ranked interaction with professors as a very high priority (Astin 1993).*** Garko et al. (1994) explored students' views about their relationships with their professors. When students were asked to describe in their own words their view of the ideal student-teacher relationship, they said they wanted to connect with their professors.

In study after study, students report that they appreciate having instructors who are approachable. "Approachable," to students, means respecting students as persons and as learners. The Garko et al. study (1994) found that students wanted equality, mutuality, and respect in their relationships with their professors.

Students value teachers who seem to care about them as people, and who show an interest in their learning. Students say they want their instructors to talk to them in language, and at a level, that is understandable to them. They say it helps them feel relaxed in class when their instructors step out of "role" and share personal experiences with them. Of course, pedagogically, this works best when you can use your personal experiences to demonstrate the course content.

In short, students feel that the classroom atmosphere is more relaxed when there's less formality, and when you as the instructor seem like a real person to them. Your students want to feel connected to you — and they want you to care about them.

**#8: *Use humor, where appropriate, to create a more informal atmosphere.*** Berk (1996) found that undergraduate and graduate students rated the use of humor as very effective to extremely effective in reducing their anxiety, increasing their ability to learn, and improving their chances of performing their best on problems and exams.

Berk studied several uses of humor, including:

- humorous material on the course syllabus,
- spontaneous humor in class,
- humorous questions and examples, and
- humorous material on exams.

Sometimes you can find jokes in your discipline to make students more comfortable in class. For example, when I present the material on Pavlov and the classical conditioning of his dogs, I put up a cartoon in large lecture that shows Pavlov sitting in his laboratory with his dogs. The sign on his door says, "Please don't ring the bell!" I'm not suggesting that you need to become a stand-up comic. However, using appropriate, spontaneous humor in your classroom can go a long way toward improving your rapport with students.

Civikly-Powell (1999) reviewed the body of research on the uses of humor in the classroom over the last few decades. She found fairly consistent conclusions. She says there's a strong positive correlation among teacher uses of humor in the classroom, student evaluations of teaching, and student reports of learning. Certainly in my own focus groups with students over the years, students have reported that they appreciate a teacher's sense of humor as a way of making the teaching/learning environment more comfortable. Civikly-Powell says that, although there is no direct causal connection between humor and learning, humor seems to arouse students' attention and interest. And there is compelling research showing that increased interest among students is a motivating factor that improves the likelihood the students will learn and retain information more readily.

Civikly-Powell also notes that teachers report using stories and anecdotes, exaggerations, jokes about themselves, and visuals that are funny. Most teachers say they use humor to help students feel more comfortable in the classroom, to relieve tension, to grab the students' attention and interest, and to have fun.

It's important to use some caution, however, when it comes to humor. In her observations of other teachers' classes, Civikly-Powell found that sometimes what a teacher found funny, the students did not. She thinks the disparity often can be accounted for by the difference in the level of sophistication between teacher and students, and by the generation gap. So it's important to know your audience.

Be aware too, Civikly-Powell stresses, that students are in a more precarious position in the classroom than you are as the teacher. To establish and maintain an atmosphere in which students feel safe, you need to be very cautious about using teasing, for example, even when the teasing is positive. Civikly-Powell also reports that students appear to be uncomfortable with teacher sarcasm, unless you the teacher make yourself the target of the sarcasm. Even then, however, students seem to tolerate only small doses of sarcasm.

## Promoting Student-Student Interaction

As I've noted throughout this book so far, the first day of class is an important one that sets the tone for the semester — for better or worse. So in addition to working to build a solid connection between yourself and your students, it's important to do something that gets your students connected with each other as well.

Students need to begin interacting with each other from the first class session if your goal is to establish a warm classroom atmosphere. As faculty, many of us need to let go of our need to make that first class full to brimming with our introductions to the content and mechanics of the course. The research is quite clear that student perseverance and success are more dependent on the relationships they establish in class than on what we have to tell them about the course.

In Chapter 2, I described a variety of "icebreaker" activities you can use during the first session of a new class. Whatever activities you choose to do, the important ingredient is to help each student meet at least a few other students in the class in a non-threatening way. If you can do an exercise that deals with your course material, so much the better.

Early in the semester, devise a way to let students exchange phone numbers and/or e-mail addresses so that they can help each other if they're ever absent from class. If you're teaching at a commuter institution, you might encourage students to look for other students from the same geographical area, zip code, or phone exchange. Whatever your type of institution, you might ask students to pair up with someone who is in the same major or who shares similar career aspirations. You can mention your expectations that students be responsible for obtaining missed work or handouts. You can then add that some form of a "buddy system" has worked out well at colleges and universities throughout the nation.

Seating arrangements are also important for creating an atmosphere that is conducive to students' active participation in class. Where appropriate and possible, put students in circles. Face-to-face seating seems to generate more student interaction than having students sit in rows facing the backs of each other's heads. (Incidentally, social psychology research has shown that morale is highest in any group in which participants are engaged in discussion.) A variation of the full circle is to ask students on each side of the room to shift their desks so that they're facing the center of the room and each other. This setup allows you to walk from the front of the classroom occasionally so that you can make the back of the room the focus of attention. You might occasionally engage the students who sit in the back and who ordinarily wouldn't participate by standing closer to them.

When blackboard work, overhead transparencies, or class size make a circular seating arrangement unfeasible, try to get students to sit close to each other. For example, you can ask students not to sit in the last row in the back of the room, or in the side rows.

If you notice that the class has arranged itself in a way that is gender or race segregated, try a random-type rearrangement without calling attention to the fact that the original arrangement was segregated. Social psychology research suggests that proximity and contact among diverse people of equal status promotes harmonious relationships and breaks down prejudices (Sherif et al. 1961). (In fact, in Chapter 4 I'll discuss the research showing that the *cooperative,* rather than the *competitive,* classroom improves the learning environment.)

Encourage students to form study pairs or study groups. Suggest ways the students can get organized and approach their study sessions. Offer to meet with them occasionally if they'd like to. A way to use "study-buddy" groups in class — indeed, an approach that facilitates bonding and enhances the quality of class discussions — is to ask students to move into four-person groups as soon as they come to class. Create some ongoing assignment for them to be working on that they can discuss together for a few minutes before you start the session. For example, you can ask students to read an assignment at home; select and write about portions they found intriguing, difficult, confusing, powerful, or whatever you choose; and discuss their writings together within their study groups.

When I tried this technique, I found that when I reconvened the large group and started the class, the students' willingness to participate was much higher than usual and the discussion much richer. In a "Psychology of Relationships" course that I taught several years ago, I started every class this way. Students brought an energy to the discussions that enlivened our whole semester together. (Incidentally, I once overheard an intriguing conversation taking place within one of the study groups prior to the start of the large-group discussion: A student was reprimanding another student for not having read the assignment. Students seem to take their commitment to their groups very seriously.)

# Participation,
# Motivation, and Perseverance

Now that we've explored the importance of creating a welcoming, inclusive, and safe classroom atmosphere — and some ways you can do so — it's time to discuss the issues of student participation, motivation, and perseverance, and what we as teachers can do to promote student success from the very first day of class. For that, we turn to Chapter 4.

## CHAPTER FOUR

# PROMOTING STUDENT PARTICIPATION AND MOTIVATION

## Promoting *Self-Regulation*: Teaching Students *How* to Learn and Improving Student Learning

Murray (2000, 62) discusses the process of *self-regulation* in the learning process. She says: "Students learn best when they self-regulate — set their own academic goals, develop strategies to meet them, and reflect on their academic performance." Many college students know what they need to learn, how to learn it, and how to assess their performance. But there are also many students who are not skilled in this process.

Murray's article discusses the research of educators who have examined the self-regulation process. Professors Paul Pintrich (1995) of the University of Michigan and Barry Zimmerman (1998) of the Graduate School and University Center at City University of New York (CUNY) have studied the self-regulation process in education. Professors C.E. Weinstein and L.M. Hume (1998) and many other researchers support what Pintrich and Zimmerman have found. Basically, these researchers all agree that it is never too late to teach students *how* to learn. They believe that if we as faculty members include self-regulation strategies in our teaching, our students will learn more quickly and efficiently. Weinstein and Hume (1998), in fact, have found that the more students use effective learning strategies, the higher their grade-point averages and graduation rates tend to be.

How do we as teachers help students become self-regulators? The researchers tell us we should:

• Set clear learning objectives for our courses.

- Make regular assignments.
- Emphasize outlines.
- Suggest mnemonic devices and other memory strategies that will help our students retain material.

Zimmerman (1998) has developed a model that has been extremely effective with developmental students at CUNY. He suggests teaching students to see the self-regulation process in three phases:

- *Forethought* — Help your students set short-term, challenging, but attainable academic goals so that they can estimate their abilities. This *self-efficacy* approach helps students achieve their goals.
- *Performance* — Help your students develop learning strategies such as scheduling study time, using memorization techniques, and outlining course content.
- *Self-reflection* — Help your students evaluate how effectively their learning strategies allow them to meet their academic goals, and teach them to adjust their strategies as necessary.

Research (VanZile-Tamsen and Livingston 1999) has shown that the self-regulating process can significantly boost the performance of lower-achieving students. High-achieving students are usually self-regulators to begin with, but lower-achieving students can learn the process and thus improve their academic performance.

Research has also concluded that *motivation* plays a big role in the self-regulation process. Some students are consistent self-regulators, while others are self-regulators only in courses or disciplines that are of high interest to them. Zimmerman (1998) and VanZile-Tamsen and Livingston (1999) offer several ideas to help you motivate your students toward self-regulation:

- Organize your course to emphasize *reflective learning* (i.e., the type of learning whereby students not only learn the material but also pay attention to the learning process itself) and goal setting among your students.
- Spell out your course learning objectives up front. Your students should understand what they need to know across the course and for each exam.
- Emphasize concept relevance by using plenty of examples to explain each concept. Relate new concepts to ones you've covered previously so that your students will see connections amongst the material.

- Give frequent quizzes so that your students can tell how well they're learning the material.
- Tie feedback concerning student performance to key concepts. In other words, frame your comments on students' tests and assignments in terms of how well students' answers on exams match the objectives for the course. This is a kind of "after-the-test analysis" that will help students know what they should re-study.

Encourage students to use specific learning strategies by:

- Helping them define their learning tasks.
- Teaching them to organize their notes. For example, you might suggest ways for students to summarize your lecture content and fill in the gaps in their notes. You could even do an occasional spot check of students' notes to see how well (or poorly) they're doing in their notetaking.
- Teaching students about learning devices like mnemonic aids, how to outline material, how to create knowledge trees that categorize information in branches, and how to create a *study diary* or *log* to help them manage their time more effectively.
- Modeling and encouraging self-regulation. Pintrich (1995) suggests that we as teachers think out loud in class when we're analyzing a problem, admit when we don't have the information we need, and tell students how we plan to get that information. Such role modeling, Pintrich notes, helps students see that it's best to identify one's weaknesses in order to be able to compensate for them. In other words, students learn to identify what they don't know.

Research on the characteristics of highly effective teachers shows quite a bit of overlap with the research on teaching students how to regulate their own learning. When Guskey (1988) and his colleague Easton studied college teachers who had been identified as highly effective, they found that the teachers shared very little in common in terms of personal traits or background characteristics. What the researchers did find, though, was great commonality with respect to teaching strategies and instructional practices. Guskey and Easton created four categories to cover these strategies and practices:

- Planning, organization, and cues.
- Positive regard for students.
- Student participation.
- Feedback, correctives, and reinforcement.

In terms of *planning, organization, and cues,* highly effective teachers, according to the Guskey and Easton research:

- Spend considerable time planning and organizing their courses before the semester begins.
- Develop detailed course outlines, with clear objectives and grading criteria that reflect specific learning standards.
- Include daily class topics and assignments in their course outlines or syllabi.
- Feel strongly about the importance of flexibility and responsiveness to students' needs and interests. They put primary emphasis on student learning.
- Stress the importance of the first class meeting for setting the semester's tone.
- Set goals for their students on the first day of class, expressing confidence that every student can succeed and the expectation that students will work hard and attend every class meeting.
- Plan each class with an introduction at the beginning, a summary at the end, and clear developmental steps in between.

With respect to *positive regard for students,* highly effective teachers:

- Learn students' names in the first week or two of the semester.
- Use part of the first class meeting to get to know students.
- Make an effort to know individual students' traits and interests.
- Continue through the semester to acknowledge the individuality of each student.
- Avoid embarrassing students or harassing them with questions or demands.
- Stress the importance of student-teacher interaction.

In terms of recognizing the importance of *student participation,* highly effective teachers:

- Make sure all students get involved during class sessions.
- Continually assess to see if students are "with" them.
- Shift gears often to retain students' interest.
- Greatly encourage students' questions and participation.
- Utilize discussions.
- Are physically active during their lectures — they move around the room and speak to their students in an animated way.

With respect to *feedback, correctives, and reinforcement*, highly effective teachers:

- Give students regular feedback on their progress.
- Spend a great deal of time reading and evaluating (both orally and in writing) students' papers and tests.
- Make specific comments about what a student has done well, what the student needs to improve, and how the student can make those improvements.
- Arrange individual meetings with students who are having difficulty.
- Often provide individual help and refer students to campus services (e.g., academic skills center, counseling center, career center).
- Follow up with students who are having difficulty.
- Encourage *mastery learning* — that is, learning the material at a certain predetermined level of competency.
- Reward students' successes by praising students for their performance; by commenting on their progress throughout the course; and, sometimes, by offering bonus points for additional work, which students can then add to their exam scores.
- Use frequent verbal praise, where appropriate.
- Praise students privately before or after class when they do well.

The Guskey and Easton research seems to support the notion that highly effective teachers teach not only their disciplines, but do indeed teach students *how to learn*. In addition, they try to encourage their students to self-regulate their learning.

## The Interactive Classroom

### *The interactive lecture.*

To reach today's students — particularly the tired and unmotivated ones — our challenge as teachers is to add variety to our teaching strategies. The old-time lecture approach may capture some of today's students — but it will probably be a minority of them. Many lecturers, facing the glazed-over eyes of their students, try to create more-engaging lectures or make attempts at a more dazzling lecture style. While this effort is admirable, it will probably prove ineffective. Somewhere I once read an intriguing definition of the term *insanity*: Doing the same thing over and over again and expecting different results. If we as teachers want different results with students who aren't responding to the lecture format, the prescription is clear: *We must change.*

Before I present the argument for change, I want to add a caveat: I do believe that *we can* become more dynamic lecturers, and thus capture the attention of more of our students. Silberman (1996, 19-21) suggests some techniques to grab students' attention at the start of a lecture and maintain that attention throughout:

- Start your lecture with an interesting story or anecdote that grabs students' attention.
- Begin the lecture with a provocative visual, such as a cartoon.
- Pose a problem or ask a question that is at the center of the lecture, so that students will be motivated to stay tuned in.
- Limit the major points of your lecture. Present key terms and concepts on an overhead transparency or chalkboard to help students remember them.
- Use plenty of real-life examples and comparisons, and try to relate your information to your students' prior life experiences.
- Wherever possible, use transparencies, flip charts, and handouts to give your students a visual as well as an auditory channel of learning.
- Periodically, stop lecturing so that you can ask students to give examples of the concepts you've presented so far.
- Present a problem or question for students to address based on the information covered in the lecture.
- Give students a test or quiz on the topic covered, toward the end of the lecture.
- Ask students to compare their notes with each other in order to review the lecture and clear up any questions they may have.

Morris Burns (1999), a professor of theater at the University of Texas, offers suggestions from the profession of acting that can be helpful to us as teachers and lecturers:

- Bring more feeling into your presentation of ideas so that you show enthusiasm for what you're teaching.
- Picture yourself successfully conducting your classes. Your imagination will pave the way for your successful performance in the classroom.
- Use your voice in ways that are conducive to effective communication — for example, speaking with inflection.

- Use the way you move in class to project enthusiasm and to connect with your students. For example, walk around your classroom and establish eye contact with students as you move all around the room.

- Think about the arrangement of your teaching environment. Check out the room where you'll be teaching, ahead of time. Plan ways to use the space to the best advantage — for instance, whether you should group students in circles or semi-circles.

- Prepare for class by thinking not only about the content you want to present, but also about your students as an audience and as individuals. Deliver your content in a way that is relevant to your students' lives.

All of this being said, even the most dynamic lecturers are today facing students who seem to need greater involvement. So many scholars in academia, following the work of John Dewey (1963) and Jean Piaget (1952), have espoused the idea that students learn more effectively when they're actively involved, when they're "doing" rather than passively receiving information. Faculty members who protest by saying they have too much material to cover to allow student participation, dialogue, or group work would be saddened to discover how few students are "covering" the material with them.

And how much of what we faculty members "cover" will students retain after our examinations? How much of this material will they actually use in their lives? Of course, this depends on the discipline of study. We desperately want the medical personnel assisting us in our times of need, and the pilots flying us to our destinations, to have retained what they've learned and practiced in school. However, much of the academic information we've learned in school — particularly if we don't use it in our daily lives — is forgotten within several years of graduation. So as important as the "body of information" we'd like our students to learn is, equally important are students' abilities to think critically, write effectively, speak clearly, make ethical decisions, and celebrate the richness of the diverse culture America has become.

Clearly the body of information we impart — *if* students take it in — may accomplish some of these goals some of the time. But the lecture format falls short much of the time. As James Eison (1999, 6) states: "... One way faculty can increase student involvement and learning is to lecture less and have students do more." The literature on human learning and memory tells us that the more actively involved students are in their learning, the greater the chances for their deeper understanding and long-term retention of material (Rosenthal 1990).

The lecture format is part of most courses, and it is a necessary part. But it's possible to make lectures more interactive and, therefore, more effective. One way to get students to do more, even within the lecture format, is to lecture for a period of fifteen minutes and then pause. During a *two-minute pause*, you can ask your students to work in pairs to compare and rework their notes. Usually you can do this without interacting with the students yourself. However, you could try a variation on this approach and ask students for a summary of the lecture up to that point. This would allow them (and you) to clarify the material. The lecture could then continue until the next pause. Bonwell and Eison (1991) showed that the "pause" procedure significantly improves student retention of material, both for the short term and the long term. It also motivates students to stay tuned in to the lecture and to take useful notes.

Whenever you use a lecture format, you can stop periodically to ask students questions. Even a lecture can be somewhat interactive if you pepper it with questions such as:

- How many of you believe that...?
- By a show of hands, has anyone ever...?
- How many of you agree that it's possible to...?

Whenever you lecture on a topic that is debatable, ask for a show of hands of students who lean to each "side" of the controversy. This technique pulls students into the topic, gets them interested in other people's opinions, and motivates them to learn more.

You can occasionally ask a non-threatening question that incorporates lecture material and gets students to raise their hands. For example, in large lecture when I discuss Pavlov's classical conditioning experiments with dogs, I ask students for a show of hands of people who have dogs or cats as pets. I then ask the students if they think their pets know when they're going to be fed. Not only are students better able to learn and recall that classical conditioning involves learning by association, but they're also more involved in the class through their participation and through their interest in who else has a dog or cat. This is certainly not a high level of participation, yet it helps students stay engaged with the material.

Bonwell and Eison (1991) also offer several other ideas for creating an interactive classroom environment. For instance, they suggest using quizzes during the lecture period to help students master the material they've just heard. Quizzes also allow students to consider their opinions, concerns, and remaining questions about the topic, and they give you the opportunity to assess the effectiveness of your lecture. Another idea is to try demonstrations accompanied by questions like, "What do you think might happen if we do such and such?"

Bonwell and Eison go on to describe what they call *alternative* lecture formats — for example, the *feedback lecture*, which consists of two mini-lectures, each about twenty minutes long, separated by a small-group problem-solving session. Another alternative lecture format is the *guided lecture*. In this format, students listen to a mini-lecture of twenty-five to thirty minutes, then spend five minutes writing as much as they can remember about it. They then participate in small-group discussions in which they share basic concepts and data to construct more meaningful notes. As the instructor, you can be available for consultation and clarification. Finally, there's the *responsive lecture*, which sets aside one class period per week for student-generated, open-ended questions. (Obviously the practicality and effectiveness of Bonwell and Eison's suggestions will depend on the size of your lecture class and the space available in your particular classroom.)

Here are some additional suggestions on how to spice up your lectures and make them more interactive:

- In the first few lectures of the term, discuss how the subject matter relates to your students' lives. Make the first few lectures particularly engaging by showing your students how learning the material of your course may be relevant, and possibly enriching, to them personally.
- To add variety to the lecture mode, use visual aids such as the chalkboard, overhead transparencies, films and videos, slides, charts, tables, handouts, and, if you have the expertise, computer-based presentations. If you do decide to use visual aids, however, be sure they're clear and readable. If, for instance, your overhead transparency has several points on it, cover up all but the one(s) you're speaking about; otherwise students will try to write down all of the points and won't be listening to your explanations.
- Organize your lectures with numerous illustrations of concepts, and deliver your lectures with enthusiasm and humor.

Although lecturing may be the most *efficient* way to transmit information, it's usually not the most *effective* way for students to learn and retain material. *Active learning* exercises can supplement a traditional lecture or can be integrated within the lecture format. Faust and Paulson (1998) say that an active learning activity simply involves students doing something in the classroom other than listening passively to a lecture.

The more students are active learners — that is, the more involved they are in the learning process — the more they'll learn and remember.

*Engaging your students — even the passive and resistant ones.*

Once you've established a dynamic of trust and familiarity in your classroom, you can employ a variety of techniques to facilitate learning and active participation among your students.

Take textbook reading assignments, for example. Since one of the biggest stumbling blocks to students' active participation in class is that they haven't read the day's assigned material(s), you need to develop ways to encourage students to do their reading. One approach is to have your students respond in writing, at home, to questions that accompany the reading. Their questions and responses can then kick off discussion in the next class session. Or, you could collect and read the questions and responses — without referring to students' names — and then have the rest of the class consider them. You could then credit the students' work in some way. Paul (1999) suggests a close variation on this technique. She asks her students to do *idea sheets* at home. When they read an assignment, they're to write their own comments and questions on a sheet of paper and bring them to class. Paul asks the students to sign their contributions so that she can offer credit for them. She then flips through the contributions in class, commenting on what the students have written without identifying them by name. When a student hears his or her question read, and Paul says, "Yes, that is a very interesting question!" the student perks up. This creative introduction to the reading, based on students' own questions and comments, leads to a livelier discussion in which more students participate. Getting students to read their assignments is a first step toward promoting active engagement within your classroom.

Many of our students seem to have a sort of resistance to learning. Most teachers can identify this resistance by noticing student behaviors in the classroom that show the students aren't engaged in the class. For example, when students aren't focused — maybe they're staring out the window, talking to each other, or scribbling in their notebooks — they're probably telling us that part of them is resisting the learning process. So Paul (1999) suggests some strategies for combating that resistance — strategies that are linked to classroom dynamics. She involves students in the process of breaking down their own resistance to learning by calling attention to the behaviors that indicate to her that the students aren't focused on the class, and by engaging the students in a dialogue about what's going on with them. As teachers, Paul argues, we can empower our students by asking them, "What can I do to foster your learning?" Paul says your students might look at you blankly at first if you ask them this question. However, students eventually start to look at themselves as learners. This technique, then, opens the door for communication with them.

Sometimes, Paul tries what she calls a *content-to-process shift*. This technique involves stopping the class and saying, "Let's notice what is happening here: Some of you appear uninvolved, some of you appear to be talking to each other on another topic, etc. What do you think we should do to get things back on track?" When you use this method, students get to identify resistance to learning in themselves and take responsibility for their own learning. Of course, for the content-to-process shift to be effective and not backfire — with students becoming defensive — you must have already established a positive teacher-student rapport and a safe classroom atmosphere (see Chapter 3, "Creating a Welcoming Classroom Environment").

Strategies involving the classroom *design* can also enhance student involvement and participation in your courses. For example, if you simply move away from the front of the classroom, you'll often notice a clear change in your students and in the class environment. In large classes of thirty-five or more students, where a circle would be cumbersome, you can divide the room down the center aisle and ask students on both sides to face the center (and each other). Students who are facing each other rather than the back of someone's head are more likely to participate in class discussions. This set-up also gives you greater freedom of movement; you can walk down the center aisle to get closer to the students who prefer to sit in the back of the room. You can also establish eye contact with more students, and use overhead transparencies and other visuals to talk with the students about the course material from the back of the room.

Another classroom design strategy you can use involves mentally dividing the room into quadrants and then trying to involve the students in all four parts of the room. By simply walking to the different sections and addressing questions to those sections, you can easily engage more of your students. That's far better than talking to the few students who sit in the front of the room — the ones who are often already engaged in the material you're presenting.

*The class discussion.*

The class discussion can achieve so many of our goals as teachers. When students participate in classroom conversation, they become actively engaged with the course material. Through a process of listening, questioning, hypothesizing, and responding, students voice their struggles with the content. As Gillespie stated (1999, 5): "...Student confusion surfaces and is clarified. Problems are articulated and potential solutions generated. Students become engaged with the material, their interest and curiosity aroused. Opinions are challenged." All of this contributes to the development of critical thinking skills, which is one of our major goals as educators.

In response to the question of why we should use classroom discussion as an instructional tool, Munde (1999a) offered the following reasons:

- To clarify concepts.
- To promote critical thinking.
- To promote active listening skills.
- To help students develop the skills of formulating and exploring ideas and opinions.
- To learn from our students.

McKeachie (1999) says that if we as faculty expect students to integrate, apply, and think, we should give them the opportunity to practice these skills in the classroom. So many studies (e.g., Slavin 1997, Borich 1996, Welty 1989) have demonstrated the value of class discussion in improving student attitudes toward learning, enhancing learning and retention of material, and promoting the development of critical thinking skills.

Of course, we must also recognize that a few students simply will not participate in class.

Some of them are excessively shy or may even suffer from social phobia. Students have a right not to participate verbally if they so choose; we shouldn't assume that nonparticipation means they're not engaged and not learning. However, one strategy that may bring even the quietest student into a classroom discourse — as suggested by Brookfield and Preskill (1999) — is to have every student find a two- to three-line quotation from the reading assignment. Ask each student to write down that quotation with the page reference, to be prepared to read the quotation out loud in class, and to explain why he or she chose it. (Note: There's a pretty strong movement on campuses these days to help students write and speak across the disciplines. This technique may break the ground for some students to start engaging in class discussions by asking and answering questions. I've found that, if students really don't want to do something I have asked them to do [because of social phobias or learning disabilities], they usually just tell me — and I would never insist.)

Many instructors have discovered techniques that don't work in promoting effective discussions. Attempting to begin a rich discussion with questions like "Are there any questions?" or "Do you understand?" is a strategy that will probably fail. The result is usually dead silence. I'm reminded of the 1986 movie, *Ferris Buehller's Day Off*, in which the high school teacher stands in front of the room after posing such a question, and keeps repeating, "Anyone? ... Anyone?" His effort is met with the kind of lack of responsiveness that is one of our worst nightmares as teachers.

An extensive body of research has explored the role of the quality of questions teachers ask their students in promoting critical thinking and encouraging discussion. Edwards and Bowman's (1996) review of the literature suggests that if we as teachers improve our classroom questioning strategies, our students will develop higher-level critical thinking skills. Edwards and Bowman found that teachers who ask questions requiring higher-level thinking often get their students to respond at higher cognitive levels. In other words, our questions must challenge students to think critically and analytically. Unfortunately, in his extensive research, Barnes (1983) found that the overwhelming majority of teachers' questions — regardless of type of institution studied, student level, or discipline — were on low cognitive levels, often simply requiring recall from memory of previously learned material. The literature on teachers' questions suggests that we need to learn how to create questions that get our students thinking at a higher cognitive level. We also need to understand how to word our questions, how to deliver them, and how to listen to and respond to our students' answers.

Here are some strategies related to questioning and responding that may improve your students' level of thinking and the quality of your class discussions. Some of these suggestions appear in the work of Hyman (1979) and Davis (1993):

- Prior to class, think about the questions you might ask to help students understand the material you're teaching.
- Try to develop questions that go beyond asking students to recall facts or specific, "right" answers. Use a variety of types of questions.
- Ask only one question at a time.
- Wait for a response to each question. The longer you're willing to wait, the greater the number of students who will be prepared to respond.
- On occasion, ask students to write their responses to a question you pose. When you reconvene the class discussion, more students will be willing to participate.
- Ask students to write their responses and then share them with a partner. This helps students feel more comfortable speaking in front of the whole class.
- Reinforce students' responses with praise.

- Build on students' responses. Use students' names to praise them when you refer to responses they've given previously.

Interestingly, Edwards and Bowman's review of the literature (1996) also found a strong connection between teachers' questions and students' questions. For example, the number of questions we as teachers pose influences the number of questions our students ask in class. In a classroom atmosphere where students feel comfortable, both students and teacher may participate freely in discussions — because they feel safe. Another connection between teacher and student questions relates to the cognitive level of the questions being asked. Edwards and Bowman (1996, 21) say:

> Professors who want to increase the number of their students' higher-order questions will first need to ask more higher-order questions themselves. Although a tendency sometimes exists to blame students for their failure to demonstrate higher-order thinking skills, these findings suggest that students can be stimulated to raise more higher-level questions when teachers elevate their own level of questioning.

As we discussed earlier in this chapter, classroom design is a factor affecting the level of student responsiveness in our classes. It also affects the atmosphere we create. To set up the classroom to best promote student interaction, Silberman (1996) suggests the following arrangements:

- The U-shape design, which involves setting up the chairs in what looks like a horse shoe so that students can see each other.
- Subgroups at tables or their desks around the perimeter of the room, facing each other.
- The conference table approach.
- The circle or semi-circle.
- The *work station* arrangement, in which students sit at separate tables.

The classroom seating arrangement will influence both the atmosphere of the class and students' willingness to enter into discussions. Without an atmosphere of trust, safety, and connection, our attempts to lead rich classroom discussions are bound to fall short. There are many ways, both verbal and nonverbal, we can promote the kind of atmosphere in which students will be willing to participate. First and foremost, our students must feel we respect them as people and as students. As instructors, we must convey that respect not only by *what* we say in class, but also by our tone of voice, our facial expressions, our eye contact, our body language, and our posture. Even when students sometimes make ignorant remarks, we must be stellar diplomats. We must find ways to correct the information by reframing it, while not diminishing the students. We must help students maintain their dignity in front of their classmates, even when we do not dignify their comments. In one of my own graduate courses in a large-lecture format, a student asked the professor a question. The professor responded, "Who cares?" No one, apart from the professor, ever spoke in that class again.

How can we foster a classroom climate that promotes participation? When students speak in class, we can use numerous strategies to reinforce their efforts. We can preface our responses by saying, "Yes, that is the kind of question that has troubled the researchers," or "Good point," or "Interesting question!" (Be careful, however; use these reinforcers moderately, and be sincere lest you be perceived as condescending.) Using students' names in class is also very reinforcing. For example, you might bring up a point made by a student earlier in the class: "As Maria suggested earlier..." The emphasis on creating a "welcoming" classroom atmosphere is based on the understanding that students are people first and learners second. Their ability to learn is dependent on their levels of self-esteem and on how comfortable they feel in our classes.

### Planning and executing classroom discussions.

Although some instructors are very good on their feet and are able to facilitate an excellent discussion on the spot, most of us benefit from carefully planning our classroom discussions beforehand.

Gillespie (1999) makes a distinction between a structured discussion, with the teacher playing a strong leadership role, and a less-structured discussion, with the teacher playing more of a facilitator role. The type of discussion you choose depends on what you want the discussion to do. If you need to address some specific points, you'll need to carefully lead the discussion. According to Gillespie, the language of our questions in such an interaction should stimulate higher levels of critical thinking — such as comprehension, analysis, application, evaluation, and synthesis — and yet be quite directive: "What are the distinguishing characteristics of...?" "What do you think would happen if...?" On the other hand, if the goal of your discussion is problem solving, brainstorming, or getting students to share their opinions, you simply play the role of facilitator.

Planning a discussion involves deciding what material you want to cover within a class session and determining what questions you could ask to tap that material. Frederick (1981) offers some excellent suggestions for starting classroom discussions. He proposes that we identify goals and values of a particular assignment and then create relevant questions prior to or at the beginning of class. He says we can sometimes break students into small groups for a discussion with clear instructions, a time limit, and some form of accountability. I believe it's necessary for us as teachers to clarify what our objectives are for the class session so that we can assess the quality of the discussion. Of course, one of the exciting aspects of a class discussion is that you're never really sure what turns it might take. Often, you'll need to be flexible enough to let go of your original agenda if what you see happening in class is worthwhile.

It's also important to prepare your students to discuss the assigned material. Eison (1999) suggests distributing, in advance, discussion questions that stimulate critical thinking about course content. He also recommends asking students to work together in pairs before opening the discussion up to the whole class. When I use this approach in my own classes, I notice that students seem to be more comfortable talking in the large group after having spoken to another student one on one.

As we discussed earlier, one of the biggest dreads of running a discussion is that we'll ask a question and no one will respond. You might be very uneasy about the silence, as many of us are. But you need to learn to get comfortable with it, and to not necessarily call on the first student with his or her hand up. Research has shown that, with each second we wait, more students become prepared to speak.

It's also important to pull into the discussion the students who usually are not the first to participate. One way to ensure that more students will be ready to join in the conversation is to ask the students to write down their responses to your questions. Not only does this tactic pull many more students into the discussion, it also gets everyone engaged with the material, and even improves the quality of the responses.

Once a discussion is under way, as the facilitator you should try to get students responding to each other. The temptation is often strong for *you* to respond to students' questions and comments, but that's a surefire way to limit student participation. Students are often more persuaded by their classmates' perceptions and opinions than by ours, and sometimes students do remarkably good jobs of correcting and challenging the ideas of their peers. Part of letting this student-to-student interaction happen involves changing your perception of your role as "imparter of information" to "facilitator of learning." As a facilitator, you need to pay attention to the nonverbal cues you're getting from your students and be responsive to them. For example, if one section of the class has been particularly quiet, you might say, "We haven't heard from this part of the class. Would anyone from this section like to address that point?"

Gillespie (1999) says that, as facilitators of effective discussions, we'll be required to think quickly on our feet and to sometimes redirect the focus of discussion. When necessary, we'll have to find ways to correct misinformation, and to help students more fully and accurately elaborate upon their ideas. The essential ingredients for success in using discussion as a strategy, Gillespie notes, are "… an acceptance of the importance of discussion opportunities for effective learning, a belief in the potential of all students to learn, and a willingness to give students some responsibility for their own learning" (Gillespie 1999, 7).

Bartlett (1999) says she has rules of discourse for her classes that are aimed at promoting open expression and respectful listening. The rules encourage students to challenge each other's ideas but to avoid personal attacks. Among the rules:

- No hogging the floor.
- No blaming or shaming.
- No personal attacks.
- Always respect the confidentiality of the classroom.

Bartlett notes that when the open, non-threatening atmosphere of a classroom discussion breaks down, she stops talking about the topic and instead discusses process. (This approach seems very similar to Elizabeth Paul's [1999] *content-to-process shift*, described earlier in this chapter.) Bartlett uses a listening exercise in which she asks students to pair up, listen to each other's positions without interrupting and without formulating responses, and then repeat the respective positions back to each other. This technique defuses the negative energy that interferes with open classroom discussion.

To develop and maintain an open classroom atmosphere, sustain the energy in the class, and promote the wonder students can have for what they're learning, it's also necessary for us as teachers to practice "mindfulness," Bartlett says. "Mindfulness," she notes, "involves being fully present to the students, to their questions, to their faces, being responsive to their capacity for wonder and to their boredom. Only in this mode of mindfulness am I able to listen deeply to students. This means being willing to abandon my own agenda and follow the students' lead. If I see boredom creeping onto their faces, I shift gears" (Bartlett 1999, 54-55).

Aside from the possibility that students won't speak up during your classroom discussions, you also have to be prepared for the possibility that one or two students will *dominate* the discussions. This is a sensitive issue. You don't want to turn the monopolizer(s) off. But at the same time, if you let such a pattern continue, the other students may very well disengage. In one of our Writing Across the Disciplines committee meetings here at Mercer County Community College — where one of the topics we often discuss is students' oral communication skills — Donna Munde (1999b) suggested a technique to discourage students from dominating discussions (she cited Brookfield and Preskill's 1999 book, *Discussion as a Way of Teaching*, as the source of this idea): Use the "Circle of Voices" strategy to get everyone in the class involved. Ask a thought-provoking question, and allow up to three minutes of individual silent time or group time so that students can organize their thoughts. Then, give each student up to three minutes to speak with no interruptions. Each ensuing speaker must summarize the previous speaker's comments before presenting his or her own views. One or two students can serve as the class "summarizers" or official notetakers, and their notes can be distributed to the whole class so that all of the students have a written record of the class session.

Teachers who are sensitive listeners help their students learn to think critically. To foster critical thinking in our students during our class discussions, we need to become expert summarizers of students' questions and comments. Rather than dazzle — or, perhaps more accurately, overwhelm — students with all we know, we need to use their questions, responses, and comments in class as springboards to inspire and encourage them. We can often do this by summarizing what they've said, and sometimes even modifying or reframing it, to motivate them to go further. We can also encourage them to work with the material in a more in-depth way, to hypothesize, to see multiple perspectives, and to draw more legitimate conclusions.

## *Cooperative* and *collaborative* learning

Instructors can choose whether to be "a sage on the stage" or "a guide on the side" (King 1993). ... In doing so, they might remember that the challenge in college teaching is not simply covering the material but uncovering it (Sandler, Silverberg, and Hall 1996, 41).

The typical college classroom employs the "talking head" model of teaching. Students are supposed to listen to what the professor says, take notes, memorize the information, and later reproduce it for an exam. This teaching and learning strategy is known as the *transmittal* model in that teachers are supposed to transmit knowledge to their students, who are then supposed to absorb and understand it. In this model, students are passive recipients rather than active learners.

Faust and Paulson (1998) say that traditional lecturers often resist moving to *active learning* strategies because they're afraid they'll cover less material. "...Weighing content coverage against active learning," Faust and Paulson note, "creates a devil's bargain: Either teach more material and have students learn less, or teach less material and have students learn more of it" (Faust and Paulson 1998, 17). They argue that exposing students to slightly less content but requiring them to engage the material more meaningfully is definitely the choice that better educates our students. My interpretation of what they're saying is that it is better for students to grapple with less content — but to grasp the depth of the material with all of its nuances so that they can analyze it — than to learn a lot of content at a superficial level. No matter how much material we're "covering" in our classes, if our students aren't learning and retaining it, what purpose does it serve?

King (1993) maintains that the transmittal model is outdated and is ineffective in teaching students critical thinking skills. An alternative, King suggests, is the *constructivist* theory of learning. According to this approach, *knowledge* doesn't come packaged in books, in journals, on CD-ROMs, or in teachers' minds, and is thus not able to be "transmitted." *Information* can be "transmitted," but knowledge is a state of *understanding* and can exist only in the mind of the individual learner. Thus, knowledge must be *constructed* or *restructured* by individuals, who continually try to assimilate new information with what they already know and understand.

In the constructivist view of learning, students use what they already know along with their prior experiences to help them incorporate and understand new material. This idea follows Piaget's theory (1952) of the active nature of the learning process. Learners must generate new relationships between and among new material, and between new material and what they already know. The constructivist model of teaching and learning places students at the center of the process and encourages them to think about ideas, discuss them, and make them meaningful for themselves. As the teacher, you're still responsible for presenting course material; but you present it in ways that encourage students to do something with the information, to interact with the ideas, and to relate the new material to the material they've already learned. The move from the *transmittal* model to the *constructivist* model of teaching and learning means that we as teachers have to figure out how to encourage active learning in our classrooms. It usually calls for shifting from straight lectures to a format that incorporates *collaborative* or *cooperative* learning strategies.

Some theorists use the terms *collaborative* learning and *cooperative* learning interchangeably, while others make distinctions between the two. The literature supports the idea that they're not one and the same. Although they share many common elements, *collaborative* learning is much more than simply using groups in class (Nygard 1991). Kenneth Bruffee (1984) says that, in collaborative learning, the teacher defines the task and then organizes the students to work it out collectively. In this learning model, which shares some theoretical underpinnings with feminist pedagogies — that is, methods that promote equal opportunity in the class-room — students are no longer perceived as passive recipients of the teacher's knowledge, and knowledge is no longer viewed as objectified "truth." Wiener (1986) adds that knowledge depends upon social relations and intellectual negotiations. Collaborative learning, therefore, requires that student groups work on tasks that have more than one answer or solution, and that require, or benefit from, multiple perspectives. Thus, the completion of the assigned task benefits from collective judgment.

*Collaborative* learning is also distinguished from *cooperative* learning in that it requires students to reach consensus on an issue. This pushes students to work together rather than against each other. Listening to their classmates' divergent views helps students realize that perspective and bias play a role in everyone's thinking. Over time, students will eventually start challenging the ideas of the so-called "experts." When consensus works effectively, students do some genuine intellectual negotiation in which they share and revise their thinking. Wiener (1986) suggests that a group's effort to reach consensus is the major factor that distinguishes *collaborative* learning from simply having students work in groups (i.e., *cooperative* learning).

Another distinguishing feature of collaborative learning is that you, as the instructor, do not circulate among the groups of students. In fact, the collaborative learning model *discourages* teacher circulation among the groups in the belief that the teacher's presence can be intrusive. Your presence may, for example, heighten or inhibit the activity of the group. So you should instead simply serve as timekeeper, occasionally asking groups how far along they are toward completion and keeping them focused on the goal. By keeping your involvement to a minimum, your students will tend to take more responsibility for their own learning. During collaborative exercises, your role changes to that of class manager, in charge of setting the task, creating seating arrangements, putting together groups, overseeing group dynamics, and synthesizing once the students have reconvened into one large group. (Note: If students have to do some preparation at home to get ready for the group task, you may also need to solve the problem of the unprepared student. Some instructors have such students do the home-work during class and then join their groups once they've finished the preparatory work.) You'll observe the workings and dynamics of the groups from afar and keep a low profile, though on occasion you may have to intervene and make adjustments as you deem necessary.

After your student groups have completed their tasks, you reconvene the large group and start synthesizing the students' work. Following each group's report to the entire class by the group "recorder" or "spokesperson" — during which there is no class or instructor discussion — you'll need to use your knowledge and expertise in your field to help students synthesize each other's work. The goal is to have students see the similarities, differences, parallels, and contradictions among the various groups' perspectives. In doing so, your students will take more responsibility for their own learning, become more open to divergent points of view, and develop a greater investment in each other's contributions. Many studies also show that students who learn via collaborative exercises have greater long-term retention of the material.

Much of the research on group work has examined what Johnson, Johnson, and Smith (1991b) call *cooperative* learning. *Cooperative* learning shares so many characteristics with *collaborative* learning that Sandler, Silverberg, and Hall (1996) use the term *collaborative* learning to refer to any learning that occurs when students work together. Johnson et al. (1991b, iii), however, state that *cooperative* learning is "the instructional use of small groups so that students work together to maximize their own and each other's learning." They make a further distinction between simple small-group exercises and what they call *cooperative* learning. According to these researchers, to be considered *cooperative* learning, group exercises need to be *structured* in such a way as to maximize learning and cooperation.

Cottell, Jr. (1996) says that cooperative and collaborative learning strategies share a basic respect for all students and a faith in their potential for academic success. Another commonality is that both approaches feature a sense of community, with the understanding that learning is a social activity. Cottell believes that students who work together become more engaged intellectually, and that there may be synergistic effects resulting from this type of collaboration. Through the use of cooperative and collaborative learning strategies, Cottell says:

> ...The ensuing peer relationships can have affective results, such as helping students to foster positive social interactions that can help improve racial/ethnic relations, ameliorate sex-difference issues, neutralize the negative effects of stereotyping, and advance self-esteem (Cottell 1996, 1).

According to Cottell, another similarity between cooperative and collaborative learning is that:

> ... They share a belief that learning is an active, constructive process. As a result, learning is not passively absorbed, nor are facts simply added to an existing schemata. Students often take new material — including conflicting viewpoints — and integrate, reinterpret, and transform it until new knowledge is forged. Thus, learning is produced, not reproduced (Cottell 1996, 2).

Notice the similarity between Cottell's overview of the notion of students working together and the work of Sandler et al. (1996):

> As does any pedagogical strategy, the collaborative model brings with it its own ideological assumptions. Just as a lecture format assumes that the teacher's role is to impart knowledge to "sponge-like" students, collaborative approaches assume that students should be involved not just in receiving knowledge but in constructing it. A collaborative structure gives as much value to the process as to its product (Sandler et al. 1996, 44).

Using collaborative learning groups within a more traditional lecture- or discussion-type class may engage more of your students in the content of the course, improve their comprehension of the material, boost participation, and increase the likelihood that your students will actually apply what they've learned. Johnson et al. (1991b) say that all of these positive results are more likely to occur because, when students rehearse — that is, think about and discuss — information soon after they've received and processed it, they usually retain more of it.

In truly *cooperative* learning (which many might still call *collaborative* learning), the following criteria apply:

- Students have clear, positive interdependence. In other words, they depend upon one another to complete a task.
- Students promote each other's learning and success.
- Students hold each other personally and individually accountable to do a fair share of the work.
- Students use interpersonal and small-group skills, such as active listening and seeking clarification of other students' perspectives.
- Each group processes how effectively its members are working together.

There are several strategies for achieving this kind of accountability. One of my colleagues asks students to submit a narrative about their own contributions to the group and what they might have done differently to enhance the group's effectiveness in working together on a task. Sometimes, she asks students to rate themselves and their partners with respect to their levels of commitment and performance within the group (Johnson, Johnson, and Smith 1991b, iv).

Johnson and his colleagues say that when groups are structured this way, exercises can teach specific content and problem-solving skills while maximizing the probability that all students will contribute and that no single student will wind up doing all the work.

Cooper and Mueck (1990) add certain additional criteria they deem necessary for cooperative learning exercises to be successful. These researchers believe, for example, that we as teachers should select the students for each group rather than allowing students to self-select their own groups. In Cooper and Mueck's experience, allowing students to select their own team members produces excessive socializing and off-task discussion within the groups. They suggest that we group students heterogeneously based on achievement, ability, and any other factors that may promote diversity of groups.

Silberman (1996) offers several other strategies for forming random groups. We can:

- Use color-coded cards so that all students with the same color can work together.
- Use nametags of different shapes and colors to designate different groups.
- Use students' birthdays, with students lining up along a wall according to the month of their birthday and then forming groups (depending on how many groups are needed).
- Use playing cards with jacks, queens, kings, aces, etc. to form four-person groups.

An even simpler way to form random groups is to have students count off, starting with 1 and ending with the number you select, depending on how many groups you want. Then all the 1's form a group, all the 2's form another group, and so forth.

There may be times when you'll want to select the groups, other times when you'll use a more random approach, and even times when you'll allow students to self-select their groups — despite the potential pitfalls.

Cooper and Mueck (1990) stress that all of the teams in your classroom must have some serious, task-oriented students who can produce a high level of student involvement and on-task behavior. The researchers also suggest that team building should be among the first activities you implement as the teacher to encourage group cohesiveness. You can do this in a variety of ways, as long as you allow the students to spend the first 10 to 20 minutes of their initial cooperative learning session getting to know each other. One way you might encourage group cohesiveness prior to students working on the task is to ask the group members to find several things they share in common. That simple task will usually get them talking and bonding with each other.

*The benefits — and risks — of cooperative and collaborative learning.*

Johnson et al. (1991b) summarize a wide body of research on cooperative and collaborative learning strategies. They found that, compared to individual or competitive learning strategies, group strategies often result in higher achievement, better student relationships, greater use of higher-level cognitive skills, increased self-esteem among students, more-positive student attitudes toward the subject matter, greater motivation and persistence, greater willingness to take on difficult tasks, and, usually, decreased absenteeism. (Decreased absenteeism is qualified because students who are unprepared to engage in collaborative exercises may actually skip classes.) In fact, the Johnson et al. (1991b) analysis of hundreds of comparative studies shows that the use of cooperative learning strategies promotes higher student achievement than either individualistic approaches or ones that rely on competition.

Eubanks (1991) concluded that collaborative and cooperative learning strategies correlate with increased rates of retention and persistence to graduation, particularly among minority students. Sheridan, Byrne, and Quina (1989), meanwhile, found that, after using collaborative strategies in their classes, many faculty reported that their students seemed to show more enthusiasm for the course, and were even more likely to visit them in their offices.

Sandler, Silverberg, and Hall (1996) cite studies that assess collaborative learning strategies from the perspective of students. The advantages of cooperative and collaborative learning strategies, according to students, include:

- The opportunity to master subject matter.
- The chance to have quality peer interactions.
- The chance to better understand divergent points of view.
- Greater class interest and enjoyment.
- Increased motivation to attend class.

Sandler et al. conclude that the de-emphasis on competition, the opportunity to be active learners, and the emphasis on listening skills and co-operation all contribute to make collaborative learning strategies useful teaching and learning tools, especially when it comes to increasing the class participation of women and minorities. The researchers further claim that faculty members who use collaborative learning exercises may reach more learners, and not just women and minorities. The research shows that *all* students seem to benefit from collaborative strategies, and that females and minorities simply seem to perform particularly well in collaborative environments.

One of the major concerns of Sandler and her co-authors, however, is that the traditional literature does not examine how gender and race affect individuals within groups. Structured, interdependent groups working on a common task may not automatically create a learning environment that is positive and fair to all students. Power dynamics that operate in society at large may govern the interactions of the collaborative groups if they're not supervised carefully. Sandler and her co-authors suggest that if students in a group project assume particular roles or assign roles to each other — such as recorder, synthesizer, and presenter — we as teachers need to ensure that women are not always chosen as recorders and men as presenters. In other words, we must ensure that roles within groups do not play out gender-based and race-based stereotypes. Otherwise this pedagogical strategy will follow the same patterns as those found in more traditional classes, with females and minorities participating less.

Similarly, Krupnick (1993) notes that we as faculty need to pay attention to gender, race, ethnicity, and class issues in group composition and dynamics, since some studies show that group work may reproduce traditional power relationships unless there is a deliberate and successful attempt to deal with gender and racial bias from the start of group activities. Cooperative and collaborative group exercises have the *potential* to help build better relationships among students who are different from each other. Many studies show that cooperation fosters more-positive cross-ethnic relationships than competition does. But we as teachers have to make sure that our cooperative and collaborative learning efforts don't "backfire," merely recreating and/or reinforcing conditions that have hampered some students all their lives, whether in the learning arena or elsewhere.

There will be other issues for you to deal with as well if you decide to integrate collaborative learning exercises into your classes. For example, Sandler et al. (1996) discuss the role of student responsibility and some students' resistance to the collaborative model. Many students may be used to the "traditional" lecture format; they might believe their role is to write down what the teacher says, and that any departure from this arrangement in terms of student participation is a waste of time. As a teacher, then, you'll need to guide your students toward assuming more responsibility for their own learning. You may need to explain the goals and benefits of active participation and group work, and show the contrast for them with the more passive traditional model. Your students may need to clarify their expectations about what participation means and how you assess and grade it.

Related to this issue of student responsibility is the most common worry about collaborative work voiced by faculty members: the "social loafing" phenomenon or "free rider" problem. Students often share this concern with their instructors. How do you and your students ensure that all group members contribute to the final product? How can the process guard against the possibility that the final product is the result of the work of one or two highly motivated students? Sandler et al. (1996) admit that there is no way to eliminate these possibilities in collaborative work. But there are ways you can minimize the likelihood that the "free rider" problem will occur. Some assessment strategies, for example, are designed to lessen the possibility of "free ridership." For instance, you can assess individual performance within each group by requiring each group member to participate in an oral presentation, or to submit a report of who did what and how tasks were assigned within the group. You can administer a quiz, either written or oral, or select a student group member at random to take a quiz for the whole team. Typically, instructors who use both individual and group assignments devise a system to grade both the individual and group performances.

Grading is always a concern of instructors who incorporate collaborative learning models into their classes, not only in terms of how to weigh individual student performances but also in terms of its role in the authority and power issues we've discussed previously. As a teacher, you still wield a certain amount of power and authority by virtue of the fact that you evaluate your students and assign them grades. Some instructors who are committed to feminist pedagogies are experimenting with alternative models of evaluation in which students design methods of evaluation for their own work, or use semester-long portfolios or peer assessment strategies.

If you're interested in employing collaborative and cooperative learning activities within your classes, Johnson et al. (1991a) suggest the following essential components:

- *Interdependence* — As the instructor, you define the task your student groups must tackle. This is important, because you have to create a task for which the final product makes sense only as a collaborative effort. Students need to believe that they're engaged in a collective effort, and that their success is *interdependent*. You can ensure interdependence by assigning roles such as summarizer, recorder, reporter, synthesizer, researcher, "accuracy coach" (who makes sure everyone in the group understands what's going on and why), and observer (who oversees how well the group process is working).
- *Interaction* — Encourage your students to help each other. This approach differs markedly from other learning models in which student sharing of information is considered cheating.
- *Individual accountability* — Create *small* groups; usually groups of four or five students work well. Give individual as-

sessments to each student, ask each student questions, observe the groups in action, assign roles, and ask students to teach what they've learned to other students. Tell each group that it is responsible for educating all of its members, and that any group member may be asked to report the results of the group's efforts.

- *Development of social skills* — Collaborative exercises teach students valuable communication skills. Be sure to emphasize the importance of such skills by discussing how students will use them throughout their lives.

- *Mechanisms for group members to evaluate their progress and working relationships* — Your students must reflect on their effectiveness as individuals and as group members. They need to decide what behaviors are helpful in moving the group toward completion of the task at hand. In doing so, the students will improve how they work as a group to achieve their goals (Adapted from Johnson et al. 1991a, 16-25).

If these criteria are met, and you carefully design each group task so that the end product requires or benefits from collective effort, you should be able to use cooperative and collaborative learning strategies successfully in your classes.

Cooper and Mueck (1990) suggest that you can even use cooperative and collaborative learning strategies within your more traditionally structured classes, without a big class time commitment. They offer several simple exercises you can try to start experimenting with such strategies. For example, you can pause after fifteen or twenty minutes of lecture and ask pairs of students to reflect on the lecture material in particular ways (e.g., have students create examples or develop questions related to the lecture). Or, you could have groups of students form teams to study for exams; you could give them review materials and then ask them to reach consensus on effective answers.

### Some specific group learning strategies.

There are many possible group learning strategies you can use, some of which are described in materials cited in the "References" section of this book. I'll briefly discuss a few of them here, though, so that you can get a sense of the types of specific tactics you can employ to help students learn from each other.

One of the many collaborative learning strategies is known as the *modified focus group*. This technique works in a variety of disciplines and contexts. In fact, it's the method I used in my research for getting students and faculty members to generate ideas about improving college instruction. It's also the approach I use most frequently in my own classes.

For a modified focus group to operate successfully in your class, you have to set up a question or problem that requires collaborative effort and multiple perspectives to solve. Begin by asking your students to think about the issue presented and to do some writing about it. If you want to, you can ask the students to generate and then list a certain number of ideas. Groups of four or five students work best. (You can set them up randomly or with some objective in mind — as, for example, setting up heterogeneous groups to foster interaction among diverse students.)

Next, ask each group to select a recorder (making sure that women are not automatically chosen) and a reporter who will speak about the group's findings when the large class reconvenes. (Note: If you'd like, one person can serve in both roles.) You can also assign other roles, such as "observer of group process" and "synthesizer."

To ensure that everyone's ideas are heard, and that no one person dominates in a group, a round-robin process begins in which each group member shares one item from his or her list. When all the members of the group have shared their first idea, each group member then shares his or her second idea. The process continues until all ideas have been heard. The recorder writes everyone's ideas on newsprint, a flip chart, or a sheet of paper so that everyone can review all of the ideas that have been offered. During the round-robin process, there is no discussion of ideas unless clarification is needed.

Following the round-robin process, you can use one of two approaches to help students work toward a final product. The first approach involves having each group of students rank-order all of the ideas from the group's master list on a continuum of 1 to 5, with 1 being of least importance and 5 being of greatest importance. The group leader can then tabulate scores for each of the ranked items to determine the group's final rankings, which are then reported to the large group. A second approach involves getting students to reach consensus by discussing their ideas from the master list and coming to some sort of group agreement (which may or may not be "majority rules," although you should strongly encourage a consensus outcome). You may allow for minority reports if groups reach impasses in their attempts at consensus.

A last step in the modified focus group technique is reconvening the large class. Each reporter outlines the ideas of his or her group for the class, without discussion at this point (unless clarification is requested). Other group members may add to or clarify their own reporter's presentation. After all of the groups have reported and students have observed the multiple perspectives on the issue at hand, you can synthesize what has occurred by encouraging students to analyze and share their perceptions and interpretations of the similarities, differences, and contradictions among the groups. This is an opportunity for a larger perspective to be created — one that is sometimes even larger than the sum of the various groups' insights.

Another cooperative learning strategy that has wide applicability is the *jigsaw* technique. King (1993) says that jigsaw exercises are designed so that each student in a group gets only one part of the learning materials, and must learn that one part in order to teach it to the others in the group. Each student's part is like a piece of a jigsaw puzzle, and because students must combine their pieces to solve the problem, each team member's contribution is highly valued.

The *jigsaw classroom* was first developed by Eliot Aronson (1999) in 1971. At that time, the school system of Austin, Texas, was desegregating and the schools were in turmoil. Aronson was called in to ease the process. Noticing that traditional classrooms were competitive, Aronson tried to apply what Gordon Allport (1954) had taught us about prejudice reduction. Allport had discovered that, in order for group contact to be successful in reducing prejudice, group members must have equal status and pursue common goals. Aronson et al. (1978) created what they called the *jigsaw classroom*. The goals of the jigsaw classroom were to reduce prejudice and raise the level of self-esteem of grade-school children. Aronson and his colleagues achieved these goals by putting the children in small, desegregated groups and making each child dependent on the others in his or her group to learn the course material and do well in the class.

To use the adapted jigsaw technique in the college classroom, you need to divide the material to be learned into several parts (no more than five or six). Assign your students to "home teams" with as many members as there are parts of the learning materials. Each home team member receives one part of the material to be learned. Students then assemble into "expert groups," where they gather with the other students who have received the same material they have. Within these groups, students read and discuss their part so they learn it thoroughly. They then return to their home teams and teach the part they've learned to their teammates. In this way, "jigsaw" emphasizes interdependence. On the other hand, each student is tested independently — which emphasizes individual accountability.

King (1993) also describes a cooperative learning technique known as *constructive controversy*. Here, students work in groups of four, and pairs of students within these groups are assigned to opposing sides of a controversial issue. Each pair researches its position, and then the pairs discuss the issue as a team. This technique is designed to help students become more informed, not to encourage debate. In fact, after some discussion has taken place, pairs of students switch sides of the issue and then argue the opposing side. Each student is then tested individually to assess his or her comprehension of the material.

These are just a few examples of cooperative and collaborative learning strategies you can use with your students. Collaborative learning strategies promote the development of student friendships, reduce students' prejudices, and enhance their appreciation of diversity. Additionally, the very strategies that help students get to know and work with one another also pay other attractive dividends. Along with the valuable impact these strategies have on producing more tolerant citizens, they seem to enhance learning and retention of material and promote the development of critical thinking skills. Moreover, some studies have reported increased rates of retention of material and persistence to graduation among students — particularly minority students — who have participated in collaborative learning activities.

## The Essence of Promoting Student Participation and Motivation

What all of this tells us is that, as dedicated teachers, we need to be experts in our disciplines; we need to master the teaching strategies that work for our students; and we need to show enthusiasm for our disciplines, for teaching, and for our students. Add to this already challenging mix another critical set of factors: Effective teachers connect with their students; create a safe, inclusive, respectful classroom environment; and set up exercises and learning tasks that foster interaction, learning, and bonding among students.

But what if there are students in your classes whose classroom behavior (perhaps their behavior is rude or inappropriate) interferes with your goals for this kind of classroom environment? In Chapter 5 we'll discuss this increasingly common scenario and explore what you can do about it.

CHAPTER FIVE

# DEALING WITH INCIVILITY
# IN THE COLLEGE CLASSROOM

## What Is Classroom "Incivility"?

What do we mean by *incivility* when describing student behavior in the college classroom? Richardson (2000) says the term is an ambiguous one. He argues that the difficulty in defining "incivility" is rooted in people's differing personal expectations about appropriate behavior.

Although Richardson's point is well taken, there does seem to be a growing consensus that the term "incivility" generally refers to the following kinds of behaviors:

- Being consistently late for class.
- Talking while the instructor is speaking.
- Drawing pictures in a notebook or doing crossword puzzles during class.
- Wearing headphones in class to listen to music.
- Allowing cell phones to ring during class.
- Talking on cell phones while class is in session.
- Walking in and out of the room while class is in session.
- Walking in late and passing in front of the teacher.
- Reading newspapers or magazines in class.
- Doing work from another course during class.
- Passing notes or playing games.
- Engaging in other behaviors that most people consider insolent, challenging, and intimidating.

Kathy Franklin, an assistant professor of higher education at the University of Arkansas at Little Rock, has been researching the history of undergraduate life for years. She says that students have been making mischief on college campuses from the first days of higher education. She cites as one example thirteenth-century students at the University of Bologna who beat their professors if they didn't like their grades. At Yale University in the 1820s, meanwhile, students rebelled against classes they saw as too demanding by throwing food and plates at professors in the dining hall. What's happening today in college classrooms is not unusual, Franklin notes. But she does point out that students today are different from students ten or more years ago because of demographic changes, consumerism, and their K-12 experiences (Schneider 1998).

There are many well-documented cases of students who have challenged and harassed their professors. In some cases, the gender or race/ethnicity of the faculty member may have been a factor that contributed to the student's rudeness. In *The Chronicle of Higher Education*, Schneider (1998) reported the case of a black, female professor who tried to speak to students after class because they had engaged in very disruptive behavior during the class session. The students had been reading newspapers, talking loudly, and passing around a game of tic-tac-toe while she was trying to conduct class. When she spoke to the young men after class about their behavior, one of them responded with an extremely vulgar gesture. The teacher interpreted the act as a defiant one, with sexist and racist components.

Hopefully these kinds of incidents are rare. Many of us who have been teaching for two or three decades, however, believe that problems of incivility are much worse these days than they were in the past. The incidence of incivility seems much more widespread in our classes. One of the big differences seems to be that professors are not receiving the same levels of respect they enjoyed decades ago.

On the other hand, I don't want to overstate the problem. Most students are respectful and well behaved. In fact, many of these students are complaining about the disruptive students. The problem is that it takes only a few students — the disruptive ones — to damage the teaching and learning environment for everyone.

If there has been an increase in disruptive classroom behavior, to what can we attribute it? There are many theories that attempt to explain the increased prevalence of incivility in today's classrooms. As I mentioned in Chapter 2, Peter Sacks believes that incivility is rooted in the new "consumer" attitude among many students. In his book, *Generation X Goes to College: A Journey into Teaching in Postmodern America* (1996), Sacks suggests that many students see themselves as "customers" of higher education. They believe that, since they're paying money for a degree, they're running the show. Their attitude is, "I'm the customer, and I'll behave any way I want to." Their behavior reflects their attitude of *entitlement*.

Add to this notion the crisis of authority in this country that many scholars are writing about. Many students are suspicious of the rules set by adults in general. Since their professors generally aren't held in high esteem by the American culture at large, many of today's students simply don't respect their professors or think much of them. Many students, in fact, seem to feel their teachers ought to "give" them the information they're paying for. Additionally, many students want to be entertained in class. And many are studying less, paying less attention in class, preparing themselves less for college, and being less disciplined as compared with students of the past.

Lest we totally blame students and their life circumstances (these are often children of divorce, latchkey children, and children of MTV) for this increase in incivility, let's examine the role of the educational institution, as well as the role of faculty members, in encouraging disruptive behavior among students.

What can we say about the culture of the college/university in this era? First, there is much greater diversity in our classes than there was decades ago. While this diversity — of ethnicity/race, age, and social class — makes for a richer classroom environment than the one of yesteryear, it may also create a diversity of student expectations for what ought to take place in class. For example, returning students — our older college population — may bring to class a seriousness of intent to learn; they may have certain expectations about how class will be conducted. Some Asian students, meanwhile, might expect a straight lecture format and remain quiet and attentive. These students may come from a model of education in which that type of behavior is expected of them. To ask questions in class and to participate, in their educational culture, could be interpreted as a sign of disrespect. Students from public high schools in America, on the other hand, may come to college still clinging to their high school mentalities; often their behavior is simply immature. Such diversity among students may be one contributing factor to the increases we're seeing in disruptive behavior in our classrooms.

Second, many campuses are today offering courses in a large-lecture format. Social psychologists have long known that, when people feel anonymous — that is, when they lose a sense of self — their behavior may be influenced in negative ways. Research (Zimbardo 1970; Prentice-Dunn and Rogers 1989) shows that, when people lose a sense of self and thus feel "deindividuated" (Diener, Lusk, DeFour, and Flax 1980), they're more likely to behave in aggressive and undesirable ways. Students in large lecture classes often feel disconnected from the teacher, and for good reason: Some lecture classes have very high numbers of students, ranging from a couple hundred to several hundred. (In the latter case, the classes are sometimes so big that students can see the instructor only by watching a nearby TV monitor.) Add to these feelings of "deindividuation" the difficulty so many students have staying "tuned in" to a lecture that lasts fifty or seventy-five minutes. Such an atmosphere is ripe for side conversations, walking in and out of class, and engaging in other forms of disruptive behavior.

In the videoconference, "Faculty on the Front Lines: Reclaiming Civility in the Classroom" (presented by PBS and the Dallas County Community College District on April 8, 1999), there was discussion of the role of faculty in possibly creating incivility or exacerbating it, and what we as faculty could do to eliminate or reduce it. Although the panelists were not implying that student incivility is actually caused by faculty, they pointed out the many ways that our behavior may create a classroom atmosphere that opens itself up to disruptive behavior. For example, faculty members who are repeatedly late to class themselves are setting an example for students to emulate. Faculty members who show disrespect for their students by being condescending or sarcastic in class can expect students to be hostile toward them and the course itself. And faculty members who ignore disruptive behavior are tacitly giving a message to their students that they tolerate or condone the behavior. As teachers, we must address disruptive behavior when it occurs. Approaches that avoid direct confrontation seem to work best.

It's possible, then, that some faculty members are setting a stage for the development of incivility or, perhaps worse, exacerbating it when it occurs. However, even teachers who create a warm and welcoming classroom environment — who seem to be doing everything we hope teachers would do — are complaining about greater incivility in their classes.

What can we do to eliminate, or at least reduce, the incidence of disruptive classroom behavior? First and foremost, we need to put into writing what the course expectations are and what our expectations are with respect to student behavior. Whether this information is part of the syllabus, an addendum to the syllabus, or a separate guidelines sheet, it should be given out and discussed in the first or second class of the semester. In the book, *Coping with Misconduct in the College Classroom: A Practical Model*, Gerald Amada (1999) discusses the importance of setting clear academic standards as a basis for evaluating students, as well as specifying behavioral standards for class sessions. Most institutions have a code of student behavior clearly stated in the student handbook. Be sure you know this code so that you'll be better prepared to deal with violations of the code if they occur in your classroom.

Richardson (2000) reinforces the idea of spelling out your expectations for acceptable student behavior. In fact, he believes that the key contributor to student incivility in the classroom is the lack of congruence between student and teacher expectations. He cites five ways that incivility might develop in your classroom:

- You fail to communicate your expectations to your students.
- Your students ignore or disagree with the expectations you've set.
- Your students fail to communicate their expectations to you.
- You ignore or disagree with the expectations your students have set.
- Your students disagree with or are unaware of each other's expectations.

Therefore, one way to encourage your students to behave appropriately in the classroom is to be on the same page with them where expectations are concerned.

Richardson also suggests that we as teachers move away from the traditional lecture format, which he says is based on a model of education that promotes one-way transmission of knowledge. Interactive styles of instruction — e.g., *cooperative* learning, *collaborative* learning (see Chapter 4, "Promoting Student Participation and Motivation") — are more likely to engage our students and discourage incivility among them, Richardson says. He also makes the case that traditional-age students are still "apprentice" adults, and therefore not fully mature. As professors, we must model the adult role and make our expectations for adult classroom behavior explicit. Richardson (2000, 7) offers the following guidelines for modeling classroom decorum:

- Make behavioral expectations clear in your syllabus. Use positive, constructive language, not threats of reprisal.
- Talk about yourself. Let your students hear what you value.
- Learn about your students. Ask about their hopes and dreams.
- Earn trust by being trustworthy. Live up to your own expectations, and be consistent in applying them to students.
- Prepare students for active learning by encouraging them to see learning as a process, not a product.
- Use collaborative projects and group dialogue as an opportunity for students to set and meet expectations for themselves.

- Model adult behavior. Remember that "apprentice" adults take many of their tacit cues from respected mentors.

- Be alert for symptoms of mismatched expectations. Even minor incivility should not be ignored, but treated as a sign that re-alignment of expectations is needed.

- Be prepared to adjust your own behavior, if necessary, and to let students learn from your example.

- Take time to discuss your expectations with other teachers. The faculty development center on your campus may sponsor seminars or informal opportunities to learn how other teachers approach civility issues in their classrooms.

When creating a statement of expectations for your syllabus, or developing a separate "student conduct guidelines" sheet, it's important that you set a tone fostering a positive classroom climate. Your guidelines should reflect the idea that you are in charge of the classroom dynamic, but without sounding authoritarian. What follows is an example of a guidelines sheet created by a committee at my institution. Many members of our faculty use it as is, while others adapt it to their specific courses. Feel free to use or adapt it as a handout for your classes (figure 2).

In his article, "Adapting to a New Generation of College Students," Turner (1999) uses a handout that talks about the academic community and the student's membership in that community. He spells out what he calls the "Seven R's" — Rights, Responsibilities, Roles, Rewards, Rigor, Routines, and Rules — and says, "...These explicit rules make student success a central concern of the course. The rules help convince students that they are integral members of the academic community. An ancillary goal: To increase the student sense of belonging and so improve the likelihood they will do what it takes to persist and succeed in their education" (Turner 1999, 35).

In addition to having a written statement of your expectations and discussing that statement in class, you should be sure you consistently come to class on time. This is another simple but important way to model adult behavior. If possible, arrive early to class so that you can connect with your students. Greet them in a friendly way. Ask them questions to engage them in conversation. Learn your students' names and how to pronounce them correctly. As I mentioned in earlier chapters, when I have led focus groups and conducted or reviewed studies, students have consistently said how important it is to them to have their instructors know their names. They want to feel that their teachers are approachable, and that they care about students.

---

# Guidelines for Courtesy and Respect

I would like to welcome all students into an environment that creates a sense of community, pride, courtesy and respect; we are all here to work cooperatively and to learn together.

In order to create a smooth and harmonious learning community, please make every attempt to come to all the class sessions, to come to class on time, and to stay until the end of the meeting unless you have informed me that you must leave early. There may be a time when you are unavoidably late for class. In that case, please come into the room quietly and choose a seat closest to the entrance. Please see me after class to record your lateness; otherwise you will be marked absent. (Please note that two lateness's to class will be considered the equivalent of one absence, and that poor attendance to class may result in a ten-point penalty, a letter-grade penalty, or withdrawal from the course — see the syllabus for details.)

Please turn off all cell phones and beepers prior to class unless you have informed me that you are, for example, an EMT or a firefighter, or that you are waiting for a personal emergency call.

Once the class session has begun, please do not leave the room and then re-enter unless it is an emergency. If you miss a class meeting for any reason, you are responsible for all material covered, for announcements made in your absence, and for acquiring any materials that may have been distributed in class.

It is important that we are all able to stay focused on the class lecture/discussion. For this reason, only one person at a time in the class should be speaking. Side conversations are distracting for surrounding students and for me. As you can see, simple norms of courtesy should be sufficient to have our class run in the best interests of all of us. Thank you in advance for your cooperation.

---

**Figure 2: Guidelines for Courtesy and Respect**

We teachers ought to treat all students with respect. We must treat their questions and comments in class with respect as well. Even if what they have to say is sometimes ignorant, we need to find a respectful way to reframe it for the class. That way, misinformation is not accepted as true, but at the same time we haven't embarrassed the student. If we diminish a student's self-esteem — unintentionally or, much worse, on purpose — we have not only reduced the chances of that student participating in the future, but we have also reduced the chances that other students will ask or answer questions. One of the major themes of Amada's (1999) book centers on the issue of respect. There must be a collegial sense of respect throughout the institution: Respect for staff, faculty, administrators, and, especially, the student body. Amada also suggests that we as faculty must be on the same page with administrators in terms of responding to disruptive behavior. A mechanism should be in place for the clear and concise documentation of problems, along with a timely and appropriate administrative response to classroom incidents involving incivility.

## Specific Disruptive Behaviors — and How to Handle Them

Depending on the particular students in your course, you could face several types of "incivility" in the classroom. Let us look at some ways you can deal with specific disruptive behaviors you might encounter.

### Dealing with students who have side conversations.

As I've emphasized throughout this chapter, it's important to discuss your expectations about classroom behavior early in the course. This may not have been necessary years ago, but it seems to be good practice today. I typically tell my students that I hope we have good discussions in class, and that a guideline that may facilitate good discussions is that only one person should speak at a time. If students then talk while I'm speaking, or when a classmate has the floor, I can simply say, "Please remember that only one person should speak at a time."

For many students who talk to the people next to them, simply looking at them — that is, making direct eye contact — stops their talking. Sometimes, walking toward them and looking at them stops their talking. On occasion, though, I've had students who seem not to be able to stop themselves from talking in class, even when I look at them. With students I've felt comfortable with, I've put my hand on their shoulder while I continue to discuss the material. This has always stopped their conversation abruptly. However, it's important for you to have established rapport with the student before trying this strategy; otherwise, the student may simply feel intimidated, and you may lose him or her.

You might also try directing a question to someone who is sitting close to the person who's talking. If you ask the student who is talking to answer a question, not only might you turn that student off to you and the class, but you may also turn off other students as well. The classroom atmosphere should feel safe. Asking a student a question when you know he or she isn't paying attention is perceived as a threat. Asking a nearby student to answer a question is a better solution, because it focuses the class attention to the part of the room where the disruption is and will likely "nudge" the disrupter(s) to stop talking.

If the various in-class strategies you try don't work, talk to the disrupter(s) privately before or after class. You can catch the person(s) on the way out of the room, for example, and say, "May I speak with you for a minute?" You can then explain how his/her/their talking during class is distracting to you and to the other students. You can ask the student(s) to hold his/her/their conversations outside of class. With students who seem not to be able to stop talking to their friends, you can ask that they take seats far enough away from each other so that they're not tempted. You can say this lightheartedly, and maybe with humor, so as not to alienate them. Students are generally much more cooperative if they feel you understand their behavior but simply cannot condone it. If you take a hard-line attitude with them, you may get them to stop talking in your class — but you may also encourage them to stop attending class altogether, or to let their minds wander when they do show up.

A variation on casually asking students who are on their way in or out of class to speak with them is to call their names during class (when they're talking) and tell them you'd like to speak with them after class. This approach generally stops the student from talking for the rest of the session, but it definitely has its risks. Everyone in the class now knows that the student will be reprimanded in some way. You haven't actually reprimanded the student in front of the class, but by calling the student's name, you've highlighted his/her misbehavior. The advantage of this strategy is that the entire class will probably be quiet for the class hour. The disadvantage is that you may have effectively stifled some appropriate class interaction by playing the "authority" role. The student you asked to speak with may feel embarrassed, threatened, and even hostile toward you. Despite the potential drawbacks, you may be forced to use this strategy in some circumstances. However, try alternative approaches first, since the ideal is to win the person, not the point.

### Dealing with students who sleep or do unrelated work.

It's tempting to ignore students who sleep in your class, or who do other work clearly not related to your class, because their actions may lower your self-esteem, and/or you simply don't know how to deal with the problem. In the past, whenever I had a student fall asleep in class — and there have been more than a few in my thirty years of college teaching — I used to feel somehow responsible for the student's behavior. I often believed that I put the student to sleep by conducting such a boring class. I also felt embarrassed that other students had noticed the sleeper and seen that I had not responded in any way.

I no longer ignore sleepers — and neither should you, because chances are their fatigue has nothing to do with you and your teaching performance. Talk to the student who falls asleep in your class. When I've spoken to such students, I've often discovered people who have been carrying incredible work loads, many times coming to class straight from working a shift without sleeping. Talking to students about their schedules and commitments — sometimes their overcommitments — can often be helpful to them. They may be able to figure out ways to come to class less exhausted. Additionally, I have on occasion discovered that a sleepy student was on medication for some serious physical problem. In these cases, the student's fatigue has simply been a side effect of the medication. I mention these examples because we're often prone to suspect the worst — of our students and of our own teaching. If we seek and understand the real reasons for a student sleeping in class — instead of falling into the trap of "taking it personally" — we can deal with the issue more effectively.

Students who do other course work in your class are a different matter. Clearly they are disengaged from your teaching efforts. You need to stop this behavior, because it is not in the student's best interest to "miss" your class, and the other students need to know that the behavior is unacceptable. There are several ways to deal with the student who does unrelated work in your class (or who reads the newspaper or a magazine — yes, it does happen!). Some suggestions:

- Try direct eye contact as you move in the student's direction.
- Ask a neighboring student to answer a question.
- Ask the student who is disengaged to answer a question. (Note the potential disadvantages of this approach, which I highlighted earlier in this chapter when discussing students engaged in side conversations.)
- Ask all students to write a response to a question you pose.
- Break the class into pairs or groups and require the completion of a task.
- Speak to the student after class.

The key is to do something in these situations! It may be easier (in the short term) to ignore a student's troublesome behavior, but in the end you'll do a disservice to both the student and the class by failing to act. Amada (1999) uses the term *benign neglect* to refer to the strategy of ignoring disruptive behavior in the hopes that it will go away. Some instructors believe that ignoring certain behaviors is a way to avoid reinforcing them, thus ensuring that the behaviors will cease. Amada, however, argues that there are so many other reinforcers of the student's behavior that are outside of our control that the behavior is more likely to continue if we don't intervene.

### *Dealing with student disruptions in large-lecture classes.*

Side conversations among students are much more common in large-lecture situations than in smaller classrooms. As I noted earlier in this chapter, the greater anonymity students experience in the large lecture setting may encourage some of them to behave in ways they ordinarily would not. I've found, for example, that students who would never talk in a small group feel much freer to talk during large lecture (especially if they're sitting where most talkers tend to sit — in the back rows of the lecture hall). I've also learned that the best way to stop disruptive behavior in large lecture is to try to break down students' sense of "deindividuation." I should mention, though, that I haven't been as successful as I would like to be in this regard: I still have to deal with talkers every semester, but I do find that I'm able to stop the talking patterns earlier in the term, and I feel as if I'm in more control of the class than I was twenty years ago.

I use several strategies to mitigate students' feelings of anonymity in large lecture. In the first class, I explain the attendance policy (which has become more structured over the years). I ask the students to come to class early for the next class period so that they can each select a seat they will keep for the semester. (I tell them that most people automatically sit in the same area anyway, since we're all such creatures of habit.) I also tell them that, according to some research, students tend to do better if they sit close to the front of the room, because they then tend to stay more involved in the class. I note that if students have a strong preference for an aisle seat, they should come early to class for the next session so that they'll be assured of getting one. (I mention this because I've had several students, more in very recent years, who suffer from panic or anxiety disorders. They want to feel they can leave the room quickly if they have to.) I also tell students that first day that I will try to learn all of their names very quickly.

In the next class session, I have students choose their permanent seats, using a straightforward, fast technique devised by one of my colleagues. Then, for the first couple of weeks in large lecture, I sometimes use a student's name by surreptitiously referring to some sheets in front of me, on which I have students' names and row and seat numbers. I also meet the students once a week in twenty-person seminar classes, where I use additional strategies to memorize their names. Soon, I know enough names to create a large-lecture atmosphere where students feel I know who they are and whether they're there or not. Then, whenever possible, I use a student's name to answer a question, address a comment, or illustrate a point using an example.

In the first lectures of the term, I tell students that, considering the size of the class, it's very important to me that they pay attention and not engage in side conversations. I acknowledge that it is understandable for them to be tempted to talk to a friend in the next seat, but that this behavior cannot be tolerated. I tell them I find side conversations extremely distracting, and that students have complained to me over the years that they too are very distracted by people who talk in class. I remind the students that they are all paying tuition to hear these lectures, and that it's part of my role to protect everyone's right to avoid unnecessary distractions.

I've found that the large-lecture atmosphere has to be somewhat different from that of smaller classroom sections. I play much more of an "authority" role in large lecture. I tell students that if they talk with people around them, I will call them by name — and that if I have to call them by name a second time, I'll ask them to leave the lecture hall. I warn the students that I may ask persistent talkers to withdraw from the course. (Note: I make this somewhat authoritarian-sounding statement in the first or second lecture just so students know that I'm serious about not tolerating side conversations. I very rarely use a student's name in this way in large lecture, and then only in extreme cases of disruption. If ever I do use this strategy, it's usually later in the term. By that time I've balanced this hard-line position, which may put students off, by building rapport in the smaller seminar classes.)

Unfortunately, some disruptive behavior in large-lecture classes is almost inevitable, unless you're teaching groups of highly motivated, conscientious students. Part of the problem with my introductory psychology large-lecture course is that most students take it freshman year, before they've been socialized as college students. In my experience, students mature as people and as students in their first college year. By their second year, in my advanced courses, students' behavior is much more mature.

There are many techniques I use in large lecture to keep students engaged (see Chapter 4 for details on "Promoting Student Participation and Motivation"). Obviously, one way to keep disruptive behavior to a minimum is to make the class interesting and to use active learning strategies within the lecture format. I have an edge in that most students elect to take courses in my discipline, psychology, and so they're at least somewhat inherently interested in the subject matter.

## It's Always Good to Have a Plan

I'm convinced that when students feel respected and cared about by their teachers, they're far less likely to behave in inappropriate and disruptive ways. However, many students may not be aware of the "rules of college classroom decorum," and some others may bring their own emotional and behavioral baggage to college that results in a lack of respect for the college environment. That's why it's important to have specific, practical strategies for dealing with incivility if and when it occurs in your classroom. It's just one of several things you can do to ensure "successful beginnings" in your classes.

But what about the "middles" and the "ends" of your classes? A "successful beginning" is great, but the atmosphere you create in your classroom must be conducive to effective teaching and learning throughout the term. So let's look at some ways to keep your students engaged and motivated over the long haul, so that they can successfully complete your course and take something positive and useful from it.

## CHAPTER SIX

# KEEPING THE BALL ROLLING
# TO A FRUITFUL CONCLUSION

## Motivating Your Students
## to Complete the Semester

Even though this book is intended to focus mostly on how you can success-fully *begin* your courses, there is one "post-beginning" challenge you'll al-most certainly face with every class you teach — and I would be remiss not to acknowledge and discuss it.

About mid-semester, many students (and sometimes we faculty too!) experience what I call the "mid-semester blahs." If you teach at an institu-tion with the traditional fourteen- or fifteen-week semester, the mid-se-mester blahs usually hit about the eighth or ninth week. It's the time when many students start to feel tired and unmotivated. A lot of our students are carrying heavy course loads. Additionally, many of them — particularly those at commuter institutions and community colleges — are juggling their work schedules and other family responsibilities. Is it any wonder that they start to get tired before the semester is even close to over? Further-more, some students may be struggling with the course material, and they may be starting to lose hope.

So I think it's important for us as teachers to see ourselves not only as teachers, but also as *coaches*.

In my "coach" role, I start to give mini "pep rallies" in my classes around mid-semester. I tell the students where we are in the course and how much they've already completed and accomplished. I remind them how many weeks are left in the term and what we still need to accomplish in that time. I offer my services to students who believe they need additional guidance in meeting the course requirements. I look over students' work, what they've completed, deadlines they may have missed, and grades they've earned. I try to speak with students privately if they've missed some assignments, or if they're not demonstrating mastery of the material. I ask these students to tell me how they prepare for exams, and to share with me where they see problems. I often make suggestions concerning study tips and test preparation to help these students persist and succeed. Very often, a simple suggestion — such as, "Why don't you try studying with a partner who is doing well in the course?" — will turn things around.

Mid-semester is a good time to try using a CAT — a *classroom assessment technique*, which I described in Chapter 1. You can ask students to respond anonymously to one or two questions concerning how they're doing in your course so far. Some examples:

- So far, what teaching strategies are working best for you?
- What would you like to see more of in this course? less of?
- What do you like best about the course so far? least?
- Is there anything you're struggling with in this course?
- Do you have any suggestions on how to improve the course?

Although it would be understandable for you to feel a little threatened by an exercise like this one, my colleagues and I have found that when we try it, the results often energize the students and the course. Students are very interested in the overall class results whenever we use classroom assessment techniques. You can briefly summarize and present those results, using an overhead projector, in the class following the one in which you've collected the data. Students listen very carefully for their own words, and they're intrigued to learn what their classmates have said. This kind of exercise will give you important information about what is and is not working in your class, allowing you to modify, shift, or tweak what you're doing. Additionally and equally importantly, the activity will empower your students. You'll send the message that you care about how they're doing in the course, and that you're open to making changes for their benefit.

## The Role of Writing Exercises in Keeping Students Engaged, Promoting Critical Thinking Skills, and Fostering Learning

What pedagogical strategies will help us sustain our students' interest in the course, and at the same time help them become more critical thinkers? In Chapter 4 I discussed the *interactive* classroom. I suggested ways to make lectures more interactive, strategies to make discussions more participatory, and group techniques to get students working collaboratively. Here, I expand on those strategies to explore the role of writing exercises in teaching your students to become more critical thinkers, and in keeping them engaged in your course.

Richard Light's (1992) *Harvard Assessment Seminars* report found that the relationship between the amount of writing for a course and a student's level of engagement with that course is stronger than the relationship between student engagement and any other course characteristic! Writing and student engagement are more strongly correlated than, for example, class size and student engagement, or student engagement and the reason(s) *why* a student has chosen a particular course. Clearly this relationship among writing, student engagement, and commitment to a course tells us how important writing is in keeping students "connected." If writing served no other purpose than to keep our students engaged, I'd still be motivated to use writing strategies. As it turns out, though, writing does far more.

Cognitive psychologists discuss the intimate relationship between thinking and writing. Their research tells us that language and writing not only reflect thinking, but also help to shape and influence thinking as well. The relationship between thinking and writing is circular in that, as our writing becomes clearer, so does our thinking — and as our thinking becomes clearer, so does our writing. Goodkin (1982, 1) says:

> Writing acts as an intermediary in *all* facets of learning by means of a variety of operations to accommodate diverse learning styles. ... Writing in content areas can help assimilate new material into a network of existing knowledge.

The results of Goodkin's extensive research — research in which she studied the uses of writing for both students and faculty, and for both personal and instructional purposes — are quite illuminating. She found that the range of the uses of writing for thinking and learning is even more expansive than previous literature had suggested. She noted that teachers assign writing tasks to help their students summarize, paraphrase, comment, focus, think through, clarify, analyze, solve, synthesize, speculate, infer, and abstract. The students in Goodkin's studies, meanwhile, said they wrote to improve their intellectual skills, to remember, to review, to outline, to take notes, to translate ideas into their own language, to understand, to reflect, to create word pictures, to clarify, to ask questions, to organize thoughts and material, to classify, to differentiate, to document, to think analytically, to interpret, to integrate, to synthesize, to test themselves, and to take examinations.

Goodkin's research demonstrated that writing forces both us as faculty and our students to think, and that it intensifies our concentration. Writing, she concluded, can stimulate further thought, sharpen the writer's powers of observation and awareness, and serve as a tool for making intellectual connections. Additionally, she showed that writing represents a personal search for meaning.

As college faculty, we seem to be universally committed to teaching our students to sharpen their critical thinking skills as they're learning the content of our particular disciplines. Writing is obviously a necessary skill in and of itself when it comes to successfully navigating the world. But writing is also so interwoven with the development of critical thinking skills that effective teaching must include writing components. If you're burdened with very large classes and heavy teaching loads, and perhaps research responsibilities as well, you may be reluctant to add writing components to your classes. If that's the case, you can still assign your students tasks that involve writing but that don't necessarily have to be graded. You *can* get your students writing more, in and out of your classes, to help them improve their writing skills, sharpen their critical thinking abilities, and engage in your course — all without substantially increasing your workload.

How? Here are several "rules of thumb" for building some *brief* writing exercises into your courses:

- Identify and clarify a writing task for your students.
- Make the task concrete and challenging.
- Add a persona or an audience for the assigned task. (Example: "Pretend you were a woman activist in 1919, and write a treatise on the right of women to vote for a male Congress.")
- Review cue words and phrases (see below) and define terms for your students.
- Produce, in writing, a clear, precise, and concise statement of the task you're assigning.

In your written statement for the assignment, use cue words and phrases and define what they mean. Some examples:

- *Analyze* Examine the parts of...
- *Compare and contrast* Discuss the similarities and differences...
- *Illustrate: Give* examples...
- *Paraphrase* State in your own words...
- *Explain* Give reasons for...; account for...

- *Describe* Give details using visual words... (e.g., "the sun was unusually *bright*")
- *List* Give a series of...
- *Identify* Point out...
- *Define* State the meaning of...

Here's an example of a writing assignment for an introductory psychology course; it uses some of the rules of thumb described above. In this case, the assignment could be for an exam or a paper:

Compare and contrast — that is, point out the similarities and the differences between — *classical* and *instrumental* conditioning. In the first paragraph, state the general similarities and differences; the rest of your paper should deal with the specifics about each type of conditioning. Your paper should be four to five paragraphs. In your last paragraph, please sum up the most important aspects of both types of conditioning. Keep your classmates in mind as your audience as you write. You may find it useful to first outline your answer by making two columns — one for classical conditioning and one for instrumental conditioning — and listing important features of each type of conditioning under the appropriate heading.

If this is a paper you're assigning students to write at home, you could add:

Your paper must be typewritten and double-spaced. Since your answer should be four or five paragraphs, your paper should not exceed two pages. After writing your first draft, please read it aloud; proofread for spelling, grammar, and accuracy, and then rewrite as many drafts as you need. Please hand in a carefully proofread final copy.

The following are some suggestions for other writing exercises you may want to consider. Some are grade producing and some are not. Some can be used in class, while others are best used as out-of-class assignments. Some are brief, "one-shot" exercises, while others are ongoing. (Note: The ideas come from the work of Goodkin [1982] and Parker and Goodkin [1987]; suggestions from faculty on our Writing Across the Disciplines committee here at Mercer County Community College; Valde [1997]; and the work of participants in Parry's [1990] project.):

*Journals* — Journals can be used in many disciplines, and in a variety of ways. Keeping a journal can help students learn more about themselves, since journal writing encourages self-reflection and introspection. Journals can help students solve problems and articulate their points of view. They can be private (for the student's eyes only), shared only with you, or shared with other students.

*Notetaking* — Convince your students to become effective notetakers, since taking notes helps them stay focused on the class and the act of writing helps them learn and retain material. Encourage your students to update, outline, revise, reorganize, and paraphrase their notes after each class as part of their overall learning process. (One brief, in-class writing exercise that works well is to have your students summarize, in writing, their own notes from the last class meeting.) It might also be helpful for you to spend a few minutes early in the semester teaching students how to take notes. (At the end of this chapter you'll find a "Taking Effective Notes" handout that you can adapt or use as is with your students.)

*Reaction papers* — *Reaction papers* allow students to first summarize factual information, and then make personal, evaluative comments about that information. Students must go through a process whereby they first learn the "facts," then do some reasoning, and, finally, draw some conclusions. You can have students write reaction papers to in-class films, to lectures on campus, or to their reading assignments for the course.

*Reading reaction papers* — Valde (1997) uses this phrase to describe an assignment in which students respond, in writing, to an assigned reading outside of class and prior to the class in which the reading will be discussed. The reaction papers are then used in class to promote student participation, with all students selecting and sharing ideas from their papers. With respect to the class in which the students discuss the assigned reading, Valde's research (student surveys) and his own observations showed that the technique is useful in promoting timely reading of assignments, greater student participation, and a higher level of discussion. Students say they have a more positive experience as well.

*Define a concept* — During class, ask students to define a concept in writing. Then have them share their definitions with each other as a class.

*Write an opinion* — Ask students to write their opinions on a controversial topic related to your course content. Then, have them share their statements in dyads, in small groups, or as a class.

*Summarize* — Toward the end of a class meeting, have students summarize, in writing, the class discussion that has taken place. Then have them read their summaries, either to close the class session or to open the next class session.

*Write a description* — Ask students to write a description of a process or to define a system related to your course. Have them start with specifics and then move toward generalizations.

*Write questions* — Ask students to write questions they have that have been stimulated by their assigned readings, and to then bring those questions to class. You can use the students' questions in a number of ways. At the beginning of the course, for example, you could ask students to skim the chapters of the textbook at home and bring to class index cards (which you supply) with questions written from each chapter. You could then read students' questions and discuss them with the whole class. Another approach is to have students work in brainstorming groups to generate questions for essay exams or research projects.

*Relate a topic* — Ask students to write about how a topic relates to their own experience. Once again, you can have them share their responses in dyads, in small groups, or with the whole class.

*Interpret a concept* — At the beginning of a class meeting, ask your students to write their interpretations of a particular concept. Then, following class discussion of the topic, have them write revised interpretations toward the end of the class session. The revisions can be shared aloud in class to end the period.

*Peer critiquing* — When a homework essay is due, divide your class into groups of three students each. Explain the meaning of "peer critiquing" — tell students they'll be offering constructive feedback to each other concerning their writing — and have the students act alternately as either the reader/writer or as one of the two "critiquers," in the following way:

- Each student reads his/her paper aloud twice.

- During the first reading, the critiquers merely *listen* to what's being said.

- During the second reading, the critiquers make comments (in writing) according to the following format:

  *Think/write/share in a pair, then discuss* — To facilitate meaningful discussion of your chosen material, ask your students to think about the topic and write about it privately for a couple of minutes. Then, have each of them share what they've written with a nearby partner. Next, ask the students to either read what they've written to the whole class or to simply speak about it without reading it verbatim. Whichever variation you try, having students first think about the issue, write privately about it, and then share their thoughts with one other person usually enhances the quality of the overall discussion.

## Other Active Learning Exercises
## to Help Your Students Persevere

In addition to writing exercises, there are many other activities that will help motivate your students to complete your course successfully. The following classroom techniques, used as presented or modified to meet your specific goals, will enliven your classroom atmosphere to promote active learning:

*Role playing* — Role plays work in a variety of contexts and disciplines. Basically, you ask students to volunteer to play the roles of characters who will demonstrate an event or a concept. Some of the many possible examples include:

- Re-enactments of trials, with a defense and a prosecution (for criminal justice courses).

- A combined case study/role play in which students are given some information — for example, data on homelessness, the educational system, or racism in America — and they then play various roles (for political science, sociology, education, or history courses).

- Having students play the roles of therapist and patient after they've studied various therapeutic theories and techniques (for abnormal psychology courses).

*"Fish Bowl"* — To enliven classroom discussions, improve students' listening skills, and keep students tuned in, ask the students to sit in two or three concentric circles, depending on the size of your classroom. Allow each student from the inner circle to speak on the chosen topic for a limited time. Then, allow members of the inner circle *only* to ask questions and make comments. Finally, have students from the next circle summarize what's already been said, and then add their own questions and comments, and so forth.

*"The Power of Two"* (adapted from Silberman 1996) — This exercise is aimed at helping students recognize the potential of synergy when they put their heads together to solve a problem or answer a question. Once again, start by asking the students to think and write about your chosen topic privately. Then pair students together and ask them to compare their responses. (Note: If you want to, you can assign different questions to each pair.) Next, have the pairs create new responses to the question(s), using and improving their original responses. Once all of the pairs have revised their responses, reconvene the whole class and ask the students to share their comments with their classmates.

*Panel discussions* — Faust and Paulson (1998) note that the *panel discussion* is a great way to have groups of students make presentations based on what they've learned together. Simply give teams of students a topic to research, then have them present their findings to the class. (Note: This technique could also include the *jigsaw technique*, which I discussed in Chapter 4.)

*Debates* — When your subject matter lends itself to opposing views and multiple perspectives, Faust and Paulson (1998) propose that you use the *debate* form of panel discussion. In this format, you assign students to teams that will defend their various positions. One team presents arguments in support of its position, and the other teams are then allowed time for rebuttal. The original presenters may then respond to the rebuttal(s).

*Problem-solving groups and blackboard work* — This active learning activity encourages cooperative participation. As importantly, it also helps students avoid the embarrassment of being sent to the blackboard — alone — when they don't know the solution. Simply send *teams* of students to the board to determine the solution to a problem together. (Note: This activity works especially well in problem-solving courses in disciplines like mathematics, engineering, science, and technology [Springer et al. 1998].)

Invite a guest speaker to class to conduct a "press conference" — Silberman (1996) suggests an innovative way to turn a guest speaker engagement into an active learning experience. When you book a speaker who has particular expertise in your discipline, prepare your students by explaining what a press conference is like. Tell the students to prepare questions on the topic as a journalist would. Then, have the speaker prepare a few brief comments on the topic before opening the session to questions from the students.

## Drawing the Semester to a Positive Close

In his book on active learning exercises, Silberman (1996) discusses strategies we as faculty can use to help our students understand and retain the information from our courses. According to Silberman, many faculty attempt to teach new material right to the very end of their courses, believing they have so much material to cover that they can't possibly spend any time reviewing and wrapping up. Silberman suggests that students will understand and retain more information, however, if we give them time to consolidate what they've learned.

There are many active learning activities we can use for this purpose, thus helping our students bring closure to the class and plan for their futures. Silberman categorizes these strategies under four headings: *reviewing strategies, self-assessment, future planning,* and *final sentiments.* The following examples are adaptations from each category (Silberman 1996, 158-189):

## Reviewing strategies

- Put an outline of the topics covered in your course on the blackboard or on an overhead transparency. For each topic, ask the students a series of questions that relate to the topic. You can conduct a whole-class discussion of the questions, or you can use any of the techniques mentioned previously in this book — for example, think/write/ pair/share (this chapter) or the *modified focus group* technique described in Chapter 4.

- As a class, agree on the key concepts, names, and events covered in the course. Create a list on the blackboard. Ask the students to work in teams to develop a crossword puzzle. Tell them they can darken boxes and/or use fillers (easy, everyday knowledge that isn't part of the course content) in order to complete the puzzle. When students finish their puzzles, collect them and make copies of them. You can then give the students copies of each other's puzzles to complete.

- Create an activity similar to the TV game show "Jeopardy," in which students respond individually, or "College Bowl," in which students work in teams. Ask students to answer review questions based on course material.

- Faust and Paulson (1998) suggest *active-review sessions.* Contrary to the traditional review session, in which the instructor poses questions and students try to answer them, in an active-review session students work in teams to find solutions to questions posed by the instructor. A variation could have students working in teams to develop the review questions as well.

## Self-assessment

- Near the beginning of your course, ask your students to write down their goals and expectations for the course. You can prod students with questions like these:
  - What do you want to gain from this course in terms of knowledge and/or skills?
  - What questions do you have about the subject of this course?

- What are your hopes and concerns with respect to this course?

Collect and save the students' responses. Then, at the end of the course, return them to the students and ask them to assess whether they've met their goals. Ask the students to think and write about what they've found most interesting in the course, what they've found most difficult, and what they might be able to use in the future. Discuss their responses as an entire class.

- Ask your students to write about what they've learned from the course — for example, new information and new skills. Ask them if they've improved in any skill area, if they've developed a new interest in any area, and if they've gained new confidence in a particular skill. Then, ask them to form four-person groups so that they can fill a large piece of newsprint with their collective learnings. Have them tape their respective sheets to the classroom walls, then walk around the room looking at each other's work. When they see something they've learned listed on another group's sheet, they can make a check mark next to the item(s).

### Future planning

- To get students thinking about how they might keep learning beyond your course, ask them to form four-person groups and brainstorm what they can do to remember what they've learned and learn even more on their own. Students generally realize that they can periodically review their notes and readings; teach what they've learned to someone else; create a reading list for the future; continue reading articles in newspapers, magazines, and journals that relate to the subject matter; and take another course in the discipline.

- To give students an opportunity to create reminders of what they've learned in your course, ask them to create small signs (which they can attach to their refrigerators, doors, desks, or bedroom walls) reflecting what they've learned. After they've made their signs, the students can form four-person groups to share their ideas with each other. You can then reconvene the class and discuss the groups' creations.

### Final sentiments

- Put (on the blackboard or the overhead projector) several sentence-completion statements that have positive themes. Some examples:

- What I liked most about this course was...
- I learned that...
- I re-learned that...
- What I most appreciated was...
- What I learned that will be most useful to me in my life is...
- What I will miss most about this class is...
- The classmate I most appreciated was _____ because...

Have the students write down their responses. After a couple of minutes, ask them to each share their responses with a partner. Then, have them share their responses back in the large group.

- For classes in which your students have really bonded with each other, ask the students to stand in a large circle. Have a small ball in your hand. As the instructor, you can start the exercise by sharing who and what you most appreciated in teaching the class. Then toss the ball to a student, who will do the same. That student tosses the ball to another student, and so forth, until everyone has had an opportunity to speak.

- Give students blank sheets of paper and ask them to write their most memorable positive moments from the class. Ask them to think about active learning activities they enjoyed, films they appreciated, and class discussions that were particularly enlightening to them. After the students have completed their own lists, you can create a class list on the blackboard or on an overhead transparency. (Note: You may want the students to first share their lists with nearby partners so that there is energy in the room and students are more willing to speak before the whole class.)

## A Never-Ending Challenge

No matter how great of a "beginning" you create in a particular course — hopefully by using some of the strategies outlined throughout this book! — you'll never be able to completely avoid the "mid-semester blahs," or the responsibility of ensuring that your students stay energized for the entire term. Hopefully, though, the techniques I've outlined in this chapter — whether they involve writing, active learning, or establishing "closure" — will keep you and your students motivated for the entirety of each course you teach, so that the material you cover in your classes stays with the students not just for exams, but for the rest of their lives.

# Taking Effective Notes

Instead of trying to write down everything your instructor says, listen carefully and make notes of:

- Key words, definitions, and phrases.
- Ideas that are repeated and emphasized.
- Facts and concepts that are written on the blackboard.
- Facts and concepts that appear on overhead transparencies.
- Material shown on a slide or in a PowerPoint presentation

**Organize your notes as an outline.** Write down major topic headings and then include notes beneath each of them. Indent less-important facts under more-important ones. Put major topics in all capital letters, underline them, or highlight them. Put key terms in boxes. All of these techniques will help you better remember the material.

**Allow enough writing space.** Leave wide margins or extra space in your notes so that you can write down additional information from your textbook, your own comments and ideas, and any references to your assigned readings.

**Study your notes.** As soon as you can after class, review your notes to be sure you understand them. If you think you've missed something or you don't understand something, check with a classmate or with your instructor. You might also want to recopy your notes, filling in the gaps and looking for connections among concepts. This technique helps you organize, outline, and understand the material better, and it helps you remember your notes. Reviewing your notes every day is a terrific study strategy.

**Outline your notes using index cards.** Write the key concepts on 3x5 cards, which you can then use as flash cards for studying purposes.

**Review your notes frequently.** If you study your notes after each class session, and your reading assignments as well, you'll be well prepared for your tests. The way memory works, we usually remember the beginnings and endings of things better than the "middles." One trick to make the middle less muddled is to make it the end and the beginning! In other words, when you study your notes, start at the beginning sometimes and read them to the end. At other times, start from the beginning and quit reading in the middle so that the middle becomes the end. And at still other times, read your notes from the middle to the end so that the middle becomes the beginning.

Adapted from
Office of the Dean for Academic Affairs
and the Office of the Dean for Student Services,
Mercer County Community College (1996-1998)

## CHAPTER SEVEN

# TURNING "SUCCESSFUL BEGINNINGS" INTO SUCCESSFUL TEACHING EXPERIENCES

Now that you've read about all of the strategies you can use to create a successful *beginning* in your courses — not to mention successful *middles* and *ends* — you may be feeling a bit overwhelmed. You might be wondering how to apply all that you've learned to engage your students and help them develop critical thinking skills.

After all of my years in the classroom, I *still* second-guess myself about whether I'm doing a good enough job. When I've shared these feelings with some of my trusted colleagues, I've been relieved to find out that many of them feel the same way. And I've noticed that the teachers who seem to care the most about doing a good job are the very teachers who seem to me to be the most effective in the classroom — despite their occasional anxieties to the contrary.

All this is to say that I see a little bit of anxiety about our performance as a *good* thing — it keeps us on our toes and helps us continually search for more effective ways to reach our students. That being said, my next message to you is … *relax*! My strong intuition is that if you've read this book, you already have a high level of commitment and dedication to the art of teaching. One of the ingredients of effective teaching that I didn't discuss in this book is your level of commitment to teaching and to your students. You probably express your commitment in different kinds of ways — in your enthusiasm for your discipline and for teaching, in your concern for your students, and in your willingness to go the extra mile. Your students no doubt sense these qualities in you.

We've covered a lot of ground in this book, all with the goal of help-ing you get your courses off to a productive start — a successful beginning — and ensure that your positive start lasts for the entire term. In Chapter 1, we discussed some of the mechanics of setting up your course and ad-dressed questions you'll need to consider to be a good course manager:

- What is your attendance policy?
- What is your policy concerning late papers or missed tests?
- What is your policy concerning lateness to class?
- What will you do to promote academic integrity, and what will you do if you have students who violate the institutional policy by cheating on exams or plagiarizing their work?
- What is your philosophy and purpose in testing?

We also discussed how you should familiarize yourself with your insti-tution's policy concerning the treatment of students with disabilities, and we highlighted some useful handouts on promoting student success and helping students do well on exams.

In Chapter 2 we looked at many examples of first-day-of-class activi-ties known as *icebreakers*. These activities will make your students more comfortable in your class and motivate them to want to return to the next session ... and the next ... and the next. While the various activities are de-signed to achieve many different goals, they're all geared toward helping students meet at least a few other students in class on that first day. You must decide which of the exercises are most worthwhile for you to try given what your objectives are for the first few days of the course. But whichever activities you use, you need to let the students have some fun and make them feel comfortable, welcome, and safe in your class.

Chapter 3 presented some of the research dealing with the "chilly classroom climate" — that is, the differential treatment of women and mi-norities in the college classroom, which often leads to their lower participa-tion and success rates. My hope for this chapter is that it provided you with strategies to create a warm, welcoming, and — most of all — *inclusive* at-mosphere in your classes. It's important that *all* of your students contrib-ute, not only for the enhancement of their *own* learning but for the benefit of *all* students. It's also critical that you "connect" with your students and build rapport with them. I'm convinced by the literature, and certainly by my own teaching experiences, that students learn and perform better in our courses when they feel connected to us as their instructors.

In Chapter 4 we talked about how to motivate your students to learn and to persevere until the end of the term. We examined the importance of teaching students to *self-regulate* their own learning — that is, to take charge of and be responsible for their educational efforts. Students learn and retain more, and are more likely to develop critical thinking skills, when they're actively engaged in the learning process. The strategies we discussed in the chapter will help you engage your students with the material and motivate them to learn.

We also covered in Chapter 4 some ways to make your lectures more interactive and participatory, some effective tools for conducting fruitful discussions in your classroom, and some *collaborative* and *cooperative* learning strategies you can use to promote higher levels of critical thinking among your students. All of the techniques we discussed will be well worth your time and effort, especially when they motivate your students, get them engaged with your material, help them learn and retain that material more effectively, and produce in them more positive attitudes about learning.

Chapter 5 discussed a *very* hot issue on college campuses today — student *incivility*. I don't want to make student incivility sound worse than it really is. Most college students are respectful and courteous. On the other hand, I've certainly noticed a difference in student behavior compared with the days when I was a student and through my three decades of teaching in the college classroom. Hopefully, the strategies we explored in this chapter will help you prevent student incivility in the first place — or, at the very least, deal with it quickly and effectively when it does occur.

Finally, in Chapter 6 we looked at ways to keep your students engaged *beyond* the "successful beginning" you've established so that they'll persevere to the end of the term. Over the years, I've noticed that some students drop out when they start to lose the motivation to finish the term. So it's critical that we as teachers work hard to keep our students connected to the material and to the class. We can do that with a variety of writing activities, active learning strategies, and even closure activities — all of which are just as important as *beginning* on the right foot, since they will influence what your students carry away (or don't carry away) from your course.

I hope that, having read this book, you take with you some new strategies to try with your students. More importantly, I hope I've conveyed the enthusiasm I have for this profession. Where else can you influence people's lives in a positive way and have fun while you're doing it? To respond to one of my student's thoughtful questions about my career choice: "If I were just starting out and had to choose a career all over again, there is no doubt in my mind that I would choose this path again." I hope you find the same joy, the fun, and the tremendous sense of reward I have found in this profession — not only in the "beginnings" of your classes, but also throughout *all* of the classes that make up your important contribution to both education and the world as a whole.

# APPENDIX
## Creating Your Course Syllabus:
## A Brief Overview

### Getting started

Many instructors learn they'll be teaching a particular course on very short notice. This happens quite often in the lives of adjunct faculty, but it may be true for some full-timers as well, whether they're brand new instructors or seasoned veterans.

If this is the situation you find yourself facing now, you might be tempted to just "throw together" a course syllabus as quickly as you can. Or ... if the course will be the first you've *ever* taught, you might simply be panicking about how to put together a syllabus in the first place. Or ... maybe you've taught many times before and you already have a syllabus you *could* use — but you're just not very happy with it.

Whatever your particular circumstances, developing a clear syllabus is a critical first step toward the "successful beginning" of any course you teach. So whether you're starting from "square one" or you just need a "refresher discussion," here are some strategies for making your course syllabus the most effective it can be.

### A critical document

The importance of the course syllabus cannot be overestimated. In fact, in academia these days the syllabus is more important than ever before, since many students see themselves as "customers" of higher education and the syllabus as a "contract" for the course.

The syllabus explains to your students what the course is all about and specifies what your expectations are. Thus, it must be as clear as possible so that it doesn't lend itself to multiple interpretations. There may be times when it's necessary to deviate from the syllabus — for example, when inclement weather interferes with the college calendar. However, you should try to adhere to the syllabus as closely as possible, because your students may hold you accountable for what you've committed to in the document. If you do deviate from the syllabus, announce the departure in class — well in advance of the change — and put it in writing as well.

Why is the clarity of your syllabus so essential? There are many reasons. For starters, if a student wants to contest a grade, and your grading policy is clearly stated in the syllabus, it will be more difficult for you to be challenged. But the reasons for having a clear syllabus go far beyond such legalistic-sounding concerns. The *most* important benefit of a clear syllabus, for both you and your students, is that it serves as a road map through the course.

In the first class period of your course, give students the syllabus. It should contain:

- Your name.
- The name of the textbook(s).
- Your office location and office hours.
- Your telephone extension.
- Your e-mail address.
- Information on whether there are prerequisites for the course.
- The course assignments.
- A description of the exams (with exam dates if possible).
- A description of all other assignments, with as much clear detail as possible.

Your syllabus should also describe any extra materials you're requiring or recommending — for example, supplementary readings, study guides, practice test books, and web sites associated with your text or discipline.

The syllabus should then spell out your attendance policy, your policy concerning missed or late exams and late papers, your grading policy, your policy concerning students who don't complete their work by the end of the course, the institution's policies on auditing a course, and the campus policy on academic integrity. Explain the institutional policy concerning how students will be notified of class cancellations in the event of inclement weather or your unforeseen absence.

When you distribute the syllabus, discuss the relevance of the course to your students' lives. Give them a pep talk about achieving success in your course. Discuss your expectations about their performance and what will be required of them to do well. Talk about your role in their learning and about your hopes for their accomplishments. Showing concern for your students' academic success seems to be a crucial factor in motivating them to persevere and do well. In many of the focus groups I've run with students about their perceptions of what pushes them to do well, students frequently say that what makes a difference is whether they feel their instructors care about their success — or not.

## Syllabus Resources and Examples

An extended discussion of syllabus development is beyond the scope of this book. But if you'd like more-detailed information on creating an effective syllabus, the following resources will be helpful to you:

- Lefton, L. 2000. Creating your syllabus. In M. Ellis (Ed.), *Instructor's Resource Manual for Lefton, Psychology: Seventh Edition*. Needham Heights, MA: Allyn and Bacon.
- Grunert, J. 1997. *The Course Syllabus: A Learning-Centered Approach*. Bolton, MA: Anker Publishing Company.
- Prégent, R. 1997. *Charting Your Course: How to Prepare to Teach More Effectively*. Madison, WI: Atwood Publishing.

The following syllabi are models you can use for creating your own syllabus.

# Semester, Year

(Class Number) Course Syllabus
Instructor Name and Office Location
Phone Extension and Office Hours
E-mail Address

This course is designed to give you some insight into behavior. Psychology is the study of behavior and mental processes. I am fascinated with this subject, and I hope you will become interested students of psychology with me. Perhaps you will learn a little more about your own behavior and your relationships with other people.

There are 7 multiple-choice exams for this course. You may take each test two times; you will receive the higher of the two scores. You are responsible for taking each test during the assigned time period in the **ACADEMIC TESTING CENTER** (second floor of the Liberal Arts Building). You will need a No. 2 pencil and your student identification card in order to take the tests. Your test can be graded while you wait so you will know immediately how well you have done. **BE SURE TO TAKE THE TESTS DURING THE DESIGNATED TIMES.** You must take all 7 tests to complete the course. Failure to take the test during the designated dates, *for any reason*, will result in a penalty of four points (equivalent to one letter grade).

The multiple-choice tests are *based upon objectives*. Your objectives booklet will be presented in class. The textbook used for the course is *Psychology*, Seventh Edition, by Lester A. Lefton and published by Allyn & Bacon (1999). There is an accompanying study guide called *Keeping Pace Plus: An Active Reading Study Guide*. This guide is optional for you to buy. There is also a practice tests book that comes free with the purchase of your textbook.

## FINAL GRADE AND REQUIREMENTS

The 7 multiple-choice tests will consist of 40 questions for a total of 280 possible points. Also required is a one-page, typewritten, double-spaced paper due on or before *Tuesday, November 6*. This paper will be weighted 70 points. The paper should be a summary of an article described in another handout. *Late papers will be subject to a lowering of the score by the equivalent of one letter grade*. The 7 tests and the paper will total 350 points, so the grades can be computed as follows:

To receive an "A" in the course: 350 x 90% = 315 = A

"B": 350 x 80% = 280 = B

"C": 350 x 70% = 245 = C

"D": 350 x 60% = 210 = D

"F": Below 210 = F

Attendance is required. If you miss class, please take responsibility to find out what you have missed. *Lecture/class notes are crucial in this course*. Missing the equivalent of 6 class hours *may result in a 10-point reduction in total points and/or the lowering of your final grade by one letter grade*. Missing more than 6 class hours *may result in withdrawal from the course*. Please see the late-to-class policy on the last page of this syllabus.

## ACADEMIC INTEGRITY

*Academic Integrity* refers to the "integral" quality of the search for knowledge that a student undertakes. The work a student produces, therefore, ought to be wholly his or hers; it should result completely from the student's own efforts.

A student will be guilty of violating Academic Integrity if he/she a) knowingly represents work of others as his/her own, b) uses or obtains unauthorized assistance in the execution of any academic work, or c) gives fraudulent assistance to another student.

## ASTERISK GRADE

If you do not complete the course requirements by the end of the semester, *and you have a prior agreement with the Instructor*, you may be given an INC (incomplete). You will have *two months* from the last day of classes to complete your work. When I receive your completed work, you will receive the appropriate grade. *Please complete your work* by the end of the semester so we can avoid use of the asterisk grade. You are responsible for getting your completed work (test scores, papers, etc.) to the Instructor and for following up to make sure a grade change has been processed.

## AUDIT

If you audit the course, you will receive an "AU" grade. This cannot be changed to a letter grade.

## TEXTBOOK

The textbook is very important for this course. It is suggested that you first read the chapter summaries and then read the chapters. This way, you will be alerted to the important aspects of the chapters. The accompanying study guide will be very helpful to you. There is also a practice tests book. Additionally, the objectives booklet I have prepared for you will help you prepare for your exams. *Reading assignments* in the textbook are given on the next page, along with test dates.

## TO SUMMARIZE

You are required to:

1. Attend classes.
2. Read the assigned textbook chapters.
3. Take 7 multiple-choice tests and receive a total number of points, which is at least at the 60% level to pass the course. Test questions are based on the objectives outlined on the handout presented in class.
4. Submit a one-page, typewritten paper on or before *Tues., November 6.*

I sincerely hope you will enjoy this course in Psychology. I have attempted to make it interesting, and I will make every effort to help you learn the material.

Please feel free to contact me in class, in my office, or by e-mail or phone if you think you need help in this course.

# TEXTBOOK ASSIGNMENTS AND EXAM DATES

| What is Psychology? | Ch. 1 | EXAM 1 | Week 3 | 9/13-9/19 |
|---|---|---|---|---|
| Learning | Ch. 5 | | | |
| Memory | Ch. 6 | EXAM 2 | Week 5 | 9/27-10/3 |
| The Brain & Behavior | Ch. 2 | EXAM 3 | Week 7 | 10/11-10/17 |
| Sensation & Perception | Ch. 3 | | | |
| States of Consciousness | Ch. 4 | EXAM 4 | Week 9 | 10/25-10/31 |
| Child Development | Ch. 10 | | | |
| Personality | Ch. 12 | EXAM 5 | Week 11 | 11/8-11/14 |
| Stress & Health | Ch. 14 | | | |
| Psychological Disorders | Ch. 15 | EXAM 6 | Week 13 | Tues-Tues 11/21-11/28 |
| Therapy | Ch. 16 | | | |
| Social Psychology | Ch. 13 | EXAM 7 | Week 15 | Thurs-Wed 12/7-12/13 |

*** PAPER IS DUE ON OR BEFORE TUESDAY, NOVEMBER 6

*** One-letter-grade penalty for late papers

*** TESTS must be taken during the designated dates or there is a four-point late penalty

Poor attendance may result in a 10-point penalty, a letter-grade penalty, or withdrawal from the course.

Lateness to class: If you come to a seminar class or to a large lecture late two times, it will be considered equivalent to one absence from class.

Below you will find a list of seminars that accompany the large-lecture class. The large lecture meets twice a week, on Tuesdays and Thursdays from 11:00-11:50 a.m. in CM 110. You are required to attend an additional 50-minute class; this class is known as the seminar class or discussion group, and it meets in LA 147. You are to attend the seminar on your assigned schedule every week. However, if you are unable to attend your seminar during a particular week, you may attend a different seminar for that week. Because we do not meet for classes on Labor Day, from the second week of classes up until the week of Thanksgiving the seminars run from Tuesdays through Mondays. If you are enrolled in a Monday seminar, it is impossible to make it up since Tuesday will begin the new seminar for the week. If you know ahead of time that you will be missing a Monday seminar, you can make it up during the previous Tuesday-Friday week. After Thanksgiving recess, the seminars run on a Thursday through Wednesday schedule for the last two weeks of the semester.

PSY 101 Seminar Classes: All meet in LA 147

| SECTION NUMBER | DAY | TIME |
|---|---|---|
| 2027 | Tuesday | 1:25-2:15 p.m. |
| 2028 | Monday | 11:00-11:50 a.m. |
| 2029 | Monday | 9:00-9:50 a.m. |
| 2030 | Tuesday | 9:35-10:25 a.m. |
| 2031 | Wednesday | 11:00-11:50 a.m. |
| 2032 | Wednesday | 10:00-10:50 a.m. |
| 2033 | Thursday | 9:35-10:25 a.m. |
| 2034 | Thursday | 1:25-2:15 p.m. |
| 2035 | Friday | 9:00-9:50 a.m. |

# Semester, Year

PSY 104 SOCIAL PSYCHOLOGY; Prerequisite: PSY 101

Instructor Name and Office Location

Phone Extension and Office Hours

E-mail Address

## POLICY STATEMENT AND REQUIREMENTS FOR THE COURSE

There will be 4 tests during the semester; the dates of the tests can be found below. You will be evaluated on the basis of these tests; a two-page, typewritten, double-spaced paper; and a one-page, typewritten, double-spaced final integrative essay to be discussed below. Each test will consist of multiple-choice questions taken from your textbook and from class lectures/discussions/films. The tests will be taken in the Testing Center, LA 215. You must take these examinations at the scheduled time. Failure to do so, for any reason, will mean you will need permission to take a make-up examination, with a late penalty equivalent to one letter grade. IN ORDER TO RECEIVE CREDIT FOR THIS COURSE, YOU MUST TAKE ALL FOUR TESTS AND SUBMIT THE TWO PAPERS. You must accumulate at least 270 points, which is equivalent to a "D" (minimally passing).

## ATTENDANCE POLICY AND LATE POLICY

Institutional policy is that you attend all classes for which you are scheduled unless there is a serious reason for your absence. If you miss the equivalent of one week's classes, your final grade may be lowered by 5 points. If you miss the equivalent of two weeks' classes, your final grade may be lowered by 10 points, or one letter grade. If you miss more than the equivalent of two weeks' classes, you may be withdrawn from the course. If you miss more than three class hours, please inform the Instructor of your absence so that you will not be withdrawn. If you miss any class, please be responsible for getting class notes, handouts, etc. (It may help to have available telephone numbers of one or two classmates). LATE POLICY: If you arrive to class after attendance has been taken, please take a seat near the entrance and see me after class so I can change your absence to a lateness. Two latenesses equal one absence. Remember, if you voluntarily withdraw from any course prior to the 10-week withdrawal deadline, you must fill out the appropriate forms, so as not to receive an "F" (failure) for that course.

## WRITING REQUIREMENTS

The first required paper is a two-page (no more, no less), typewritten, double-spaced research summary paper (stapled and NOT IN A FOLDER) due on or before 3/08 or 3/09 depending on when your class meets. Please sign the back of the paper only! The assignment involves summarizing any two articles from scholarly journals. You will be writing a one-page summary of each article and then stapling the two pages together. The articles must relate to the content of the course in some way. The articles must be selected from psychology journals or from professional journals in other fields – e.g., nursing – and must be current (1995-present). Books, encyclope-dias, and popular magazines are <u>not acceptable</u> sources of information. Internet sources must be scholarly and documented. You should use the APA (American Psychological Association) format for your paper. This format will be explained in class, and a handout called "APA Format" will be distributed in class.

<u>Papers submitted after the deadline will have the same late penalty as a make-up examination</u>. In order to receive credit for the course, you must take all 4 tests, submit a two-page research summary paper, a one-page final integrative essay, and achieve at least 60 percent of the total possible points for the course.

To write the research summary paper, you may want to use the journals in psychology.

OUR INSTITUTION HAS THE FOLLOWING PSYCHOLOGY JOURNALS:

*American Psychologist*

*Child Development*

*Contemporary Psychology*

*Developmental Psychology*

*Journal of Abnormal Psychology*

*Journal of Applied Psychology*

*Journal of Educational Psychology*

*Journal of Personality and Social Psychology*

*Journal of Psychology*

*Journal of Social Psychology*

*Psychological Abstracts*

*Teaching of Psychology*

Access to full-text journal articles in psychology is limited on the Internet. There will be a separate handout explaining how to use the Internet if you choose to do your research online.

The short research summary paper should follow the psychology shorthand format for citing references. Your paper should include REFERENCES at the end of the body of the paper. This reference list should give the following information: author(s), title, name of journal, volume, and date of publication. Use your textbook or the journals themselves for examples of citing books, journal articles, etc, or see my APA format handout.

In the body of your paper, you need not footnote in the traditional way. Instead, if you quote directly, indent and single-space the quote. Do not use quotation marks. Following the quote, put parentheses, the author's name, the date of publication and the page number.

If you do not quote directly but use someone else's idea, you may follow the idea with parentheses as above. Or, within your paper you may say, for example: "As Jones, 1999, points out..." or "In an article by Jones, 2000, it was suggested that..." There are several variations you may use.

This paper will be judged on the quality of the presentation of the material: coherence, organization, and clarity. You have nine weeks to prepare this paper; it is expected to be a scholarly and professional job. This paper is worth 75 points toward your final grade.

## FINAL CRITICAL THINKING INTEGRATIVE EXERCISE (Second Paper Due)

Please write (double-spaced, typed) a one-page reflective essay discussing how the perspective of a "social psychologist" differs from that of other psychologists. In your essay, you will be explaining an essential theme underlying many of the topics of this course. Essentially, you will be describing a "social psychological perspective." This paper is due on or before 4/20 or 4/21 (depending on when your class meets) and is worth 75 points toward your final grade. Late papers will be subject to a late penalty equivalent to one letter grade.

## TEXTBOOK:

*Social Psychology: The Heart and the Mind.* Aronson, E., Wilson, T., and Akert, R., Addison-Wesley-Longman Publishers, Third Edition, 1999.

CHAPTERS

1. Introduction to Social Psychology

2. Methodology: The Process of Doing Research

3. Social Cognition: How We Think About the Social World

TEST I:   Ch. 1, 2, 3             Week 4
2/10-2/16

4. Social Perception: How We Come to Understand Other People

5. Self-Understanding: How We Come to Know Ourselves

6. Self-Justification and the Need to Maintain Self-Esteem

TEST II: Ch. 4, 5, 6           Week 7
3/2-3/8

10. Interpersonal Attraction: From First Impressions to Close Relationships

11. Prosocial Behavior: Why Do People Help?

7. Attitudes and Attitude Change

13. Prejudice: Causes and Cures

TEST III: Ch. 10, 11, 7, 13     Week 11
4/6-4/12

8. Conformity: Influencing Behavior

9. Group Processes

12. Aggression: Why We Hurt Other People

Module 1: Social Psychology and Health

TEST IV: Ch. 8, 9, 12, Module 1    Week 15
5/04-5/09

## TESTS

There will be 4 multiple-choice tests, occurring in the Testing Center, LA 215. Failure to take the test during the designated dates, for any reason, will mean you will need permission to take a make-up examination, with a starting grade one letter grade lower than your exam merits. Tests will be based on your reading, on films, and on lecture/discussion classes.

ALL EXAMS MUST BE TAKEN IN THE TESTING CENTER, LA 215, during these designated dates:

| | |
|---|---|
| Test I | 2/10 – 2/16 |
| Test II | 3/2 – 3/8 |
| Test III | 4/6 – 4/12 |
| Test IV | 5/04 – 5/09 |

Summary papers will be due on 3/8 or 3/9 (depending on when your class meets).

Final papers will be due on 4/20 or 4/21 (depending on when your class meets).

## ACADEMIC INTEGRITY

*Academic Integrity* refers to the "integral" quality of the search for knowledge that a student undertakes. The work a student produces, therefore, ought to be wholly his or hers; it should result completely from the student's own efforts.

A student will be guilty of violating Academic Integrity if he/she a) knowingly represents work of others as his/her own, b) uses or obtains unauthorized assistance in the execution of any academic work, or c) gives fraudulent assistance to another student.

## ASTERISK GRADE POLICY

If you do not complete the course requirements by the end of the semester, and you have a prior agreement with the Instructor, you may be given an I* (incomplete). You will have two months from the last day of classes to complete your work. When I receive your completed work, you will receive the appropriate grade. Please complete your work by the end of the semester so we can avoid use of the asterisk grade. You are responsible for getting your completed work (test scores, papers, etc.) to the Instructor and for following up to make sure a grade change has been processed. If you do not complete the work, I* automatically changes to an "F."

## AUDIT

If you audit the course, you will receive an "AU" grade. This cannot be changed to a letter grade.

# FINAL GRADE DETERMINATION

| Test I | 60 Questions | 60 Points |
|--------|--------------|-----------|
| II | 70 questions | 70 points |
| III | 90 questions | 90 points |
| IV | 80 questions | <u>80 points</u> |
| Exam TOTAL = | | 300 points |
| Two-page research summary paper = | | 75 points |
| One-page final integrative essay = | | 75 points |
| | | 450 Total points |

450 x 90% = 405  = A        450 x 80% = 360 = B

450 x 70% = 315 = C        450 x 60% = 270 = D

<u>Below  270 = F</u>

# HELPFUL TEACHING RESOURCES

## Books

Angelo, T.A., and Cross, K.P. 1993. *Classroom Assessment Techniques: A Handbook for College Teachers,* Second Edition. San Francisco: Jossey-Bass.

Bonwell, C.C., and Eisen, J.A. 1991. *Active Learning: Creating Excitement in the Classroom. ASHE-ERIC Higher Education Report No. 1.* Washington, DC: George Washington University School of Education and Human Development.

Bruffee, K.A. 1993. *Collaborative Learning: Higher Education, Interdependence, and the Authority of Knowledge.* Baltimore, MD: Johns Hopkins University Press.

Magnan, R. 1990. *147 Practical Tips for Teaching Professors.* Madison, WI: Atwood Publishing.

McKeachie, W.J. 1994. *Teaching Tips,* Ninth Edition. Lexington, MA: D.C. Heath.

Prégent, R. 1997. *Charting Your Course: How to Prepare to Teach More Effectively.* Madison, WI: Atwood Publishing.

Silberman, M. 1996. *Active Learning: 101 Strategies to Teach Any Subject.* Boston: Allyn & Bacon.

Wienbroer, D.R. 2001. *Rules of Thumb for Online Research.* New York: McGraw-Hill Publishers. (Online see: www.mhhe.com/socscience/english/weinbroer/)

## Periodicals

*Journal of College Student Retention: Research, Theory, & Practice*
www.collegeways.com/retention_journal.htm

*College Student Journal*
journals825.home.mindspring.com/csj.html

*Journal of College Student Development*
www.jcsd.appstate.edu

*The Review of Higher Education*
www.press.jhu.edu/press/journals/rhe

*Community College Journal*
    www.aacc.nche.edu/books/journal/journalindex.htm
*Change: The Magazine of Higher Learning*
    www.aahe.org/change
*The Teaching Professor*
    www.magnapubs.com/Newsletters/Ttp/main.html
*The Chronicle of Higher Education*
    www.chronicle.com
*Journal on Excellence in College Teaching*
    ject.lib.muohio.edu

## Online Resources

*Electronic Journal on Excellence in College Teaching* (ject.lib.muohio.edu) – "The Journal on Excellence in College Teaching is a peer-reviewed journal published at Miami University by and for faculty at universities and two-and four-year colleges to increase student learning through effective teaching, interest in and enthusiasm for the profession of teaching, and communication among faculty about their classroom experiences. It answers Ernest Boyer's (1990) call for a forum to present the scholarship of teaching and learning. *The Journal* provides a scholarly, written forum for discussion by faculty about all areas affecting teaching and learning, and gives faculty the opportunity to share proven, innovative pedagogies and thoughtful, inspirational insights about teaching." *The Journal* offers free access to abstracts on a broad range of topics of interest to college teachers. Getting full-text articles requires a paid subscription.

*The Educational Resources Information Center* (ERIC) Clearinghouse on Assessment and Evaluation (www.ericae.net) – ERIC is a project of the National Library of Education, U.S. Department of Education, directed by the Department of Measurement, Statistics, and Evaluation at the University of Maryland in College Park: "We provide balanced information concerning educational assessment, evaluation, and research methodology. We provide resources to encourage the responsible use of educational data. We promote the best resources within our scope." You can hit a link called "Library" and have access to books and articles from across the Internet, an online journal, and ERIC digests. "Search Eric" (searcheric.org), another link, allows you to search over one million abstracts of education articles and resources, and these are now available in Spanish and German in addition to English. The online journal is called *Practical Assessment, Research, and Evaluation* (www.ericae.net/pare). It's a peer-reviewed electronic journal: "Its purpose is to provide education professionals access to refereed articles that can have a positive impact on assessment, research, evaluation, and teaching practice...Manuscripts published in *Practical Assessment, Research and Evaluation* are scholarly syntheses of research and ideas about issues and practices in education."

*National Education Association's Higher Education Program* (www.nea.org/he) – Two of the program's publications may be useful: *The Advocate,* which is available in print and online; and *Thought and Action,* a journal dealing with a broad range of topics in higher education. The Fall 2000 issue is a retrospection of the past sixteen years, reprinting articles from writers such as Ernest Boyer and

Ralph Nader that trace the changes in academia over the last decades of the twenti-eth century.

*DiversityWeb* (www.diversityweb.org) – DiversityWeb was developed by the Association of American Colleges and Universities and the University of Maryland, in collaboration with Diversity Connections and Diverse CD. Resources on Diver-sityWeb are organized around seven "Campus Diversity Priorities":

- Institutional Vision, Leadership, and Systematic Change
- Student Involvement and Development
- Campus and Community Connections
- Research Evaluation and Impact
- Curriculum Transformation
- Faculty and Staff Involvement
- Policy and Legal Issues.

You may discuss diversity in higher education through the DiversityWeb listserv (www.diversityweb.org/WorkRooms/listserv.html). You can also click on *Diversity Digest* (www.diversityweb.org/Digest), a publication focusing on faculty involvement.

## Professional Organizations

National Education Association's Higher Education Program
www.nea.org/he

American Association of Colleges and Universities
www.aacu-edu.org

American Council on Education
www.acenet.edu

American Association for Higher Education
www.aahe.org

Council of Colleges of Arts and Sciences
www.ccas.net

American Association of Community Colleges
www.aacc.nche.edu

## Professional Conferences

*Events in Academe*, a semi-annual publication of *The Chronicle of Higher Educa-tion*, announces conferences and meetings; institutes; and fellowships, grants, pa-pers, and prizes for the year. The February issue covers the upcoming spring and summer while the August issue covers the upcoming fall and winter.

Lilly Conferences on College and University Teaching
www.iats.com

AAHE National Conference on Higher Education
www.aahe.org

AAHE Summer Academy
www.aahe.org

Foundation/Center for Critical Thinking (offers national conferences, a national academy, an international conference, and workshops at campus sites)
www.criticalthinking.org

Council on International Educational Exchange (offers international faculty development summer seminars)
www.ciee.org/ifds

National Conference on Race and Ethnicity in American Higher Education
www.occe.ou.edu/NCORE

The Center for the Study of Diversity in Teaching and Learning in Higher Education (offers a national conference)
www.TeachLearn.fhda.edu

The Center for the Advancement of Teaching and Learning at Florida Community College (co-sponsors the annual International Conference on College Teaching and Learning in Jacksonville)
www.teachlearn.org

Collaboration for the Advancement of College Teaching and Learning (an alliance of colleges and universities that supports and promotes outstanding college teaching, sponsoring semi-annual conferences on teaching and learning)
www.collab.org

Your discipline's national organization may have subgroups that deal with college teaching. For example, among its many publications, the American Psychological Association (www.apa.org) publishes the journal *American Psychologist* and the monthly magazine *Monitor on Psychology*, both of which announce national, international, and regional meetings and conferences. Some of these conferences deal with college teaching. In addition, APA publishes a bi-monthly newsletter, *Psychology Teachers Network*, for high school and college psychology teachers.

Similarly, the Community College Humanities Association (www.ccha-assoc. org) sponsors national and regional conferences on various themes related to college teaching.

# REFERENCES

Allport, G.W. 1954. *The Nature of Prejudice*. Reading, MA: Addison-Wesley Publishing Company.

Amada, G. 1999. *Coping with Misconduct in the College Classroom: A Practical Model*. Asheville, NC: College Administration Publications, Inc.

Angelo, T.A., and Cross, K.P. 1993. *Classroom Assessment Techniques: A Handbook for College Teachers*, Second Edition. San Francisco: Jossey-Bass, Publishers.

Aronson, E., Blaney, N., Stephin, C., Sikes, J., and Snapp, M. 1978. *The Jigsaw Classroom*. Beverly Hills, CA: Sage Publishing.

Aronson, E., Wilson, T.D., and Akert, R.M. 1999. *Social Psychology*, Third Edition. Englewood Cliffs, NJ: Prentice Hall.

Astin, A.W. 1993. *What Matters in College? Four Critical Years Revisited*. San Francisco: Jossey-Bass, Publishers.

Bank, B.J., Biddle, B.J., and Slavings, R.L. 1990. Effects of peer, faculty, and parental influences on student persistence. *The Sociological Quarterly*, 63, 208-225.

Barnes, C.P. 1983. Questioning in college classrooms. In C.L. Ellner (Ed.), *Studies of College Teaching*. Lexington, MA: Lexington Books, 61-81.

Bartlett, E.A. 1999. Keeping wonder alive in today's college classrooms. *Thought and Action*, 15(2), 47-57.

Bem, S.L. 1993. *The Lenses of Gender: Transforming the Debate on Sexual Inequality*. New Haven, CT: Yale University Press.

Berk, R. 1996. Student ratings of 10 strategies for using humor in college teaching. *Journal on Excellence in College Teaching*, 7(3), 71-92.

Berko, R.M., Aitken, J., with Wolvin, A.D., and Wolvin, D.R. 1998. *Handbook of Instructional Options with Test Items. Communicating: A Social and Career Focus*, Seventh Edition. New York: Houghton Mifflin Company.

Boll, R.N., and Parkman, B. 1988. Taking roll: An instructional innovation. *Innovation Abstracts*, 10(18), 2.

Bonwell, C.C., and Eison, J.A. 1991. *Active Learning: Creating Excitement in the Classroom. ASHE-ERIC Higher Education Report No. 1.* Washington, DC: George Washington University School of Education and Human Development.

Borich, G.D. 1996. *Effective Teaching Methods.* Englewood Cliffs, NJ: Prentice Hall.

Boyd, R.T.C. 1988. Improving your test-taking skills. *Practical Assessment, Research & Evaluation, 1*(2), 1-4.

Boyer, E.L. 1990. *Scholarship Reconsidered: Priorities of the Professorate.* Princeton, NJ: Carnegie Foundation for the Advancement of Teaching.

Brinckerhoff, L.C. 1991. *College Students With Learning Disabilities*, Second Edition (brochure). Boston: Association on Higher Education and Disability.

Brookfield, S., and Preskill, S. 1999. *Discussion as a Way of Teaching: Tools and Techniques for Democratic Classrooms.* San Francisco: Jossey-Bass, Publishers.

Bruffee, K.A. 1984. Collaborative learning and the "conversion of mankind." *College English, 46,* 635-652.

Burns, M.U. 1999. All the world's a stage. *Advocate: For NEA Members in Higher Education,* October, 5-8.

Carr, P.A. (undated). *Passport to Success.* West Windsor, NJ: Mercer County Community College Press.

Cate, R., and Sugawara, A.I. 1986. Sex role orientation and dimensions of self-esteem among middle adolescents. *Sex Roles, 15*(3/4), 145-158.

Civikly-Powell, J. 1999. Taking humor seriously. *Advocate: For NEA Members in Higher Education,* August, 5-8.

Civikly, J.M. 1986. Humor and the enjoyment of college teaching. In J.M. Civikly (Ed.), *Communicating in College Classrooms. New Directions for Teaching and Learning, 26.* San Francisco: Jossey-Bass, Publishers, 61-70.

Constantinople, A., Cornelius, R., and Gray, J. 1988. The chilly climate: Fact or artifact? *Journal of Higher Education, 59*(5), 527-550.

Cooper, J.L., and Mueck, R. 1990. Student involvement in learning: Cooperative learning and college instruction. *Journal on Excellence in College Teaching, 1,* 68-76.

Cornelius, R.R., Gray, J.M., and Constantinople, A.P. 1990. Student-faculty interaction in the college classroom. *Journal of Research and Development in Education, 23*(4), 189-197.

Côté, J.E. 1996. Identity: A multidimensional analysis. In G.R. Adams, R. Montemayor, and T.P. Gullotta (Eds.), *Psychosocial Development During Adolescence: Progress in Developmental Contextualism.* Thousand Oaks, CA: Sage, 130-164.

Cottell, P.G., Jr. 1996. A union of collaborative learning and cooperative learning: An overview of this issue. *Journal on Excellence in College Teaching, 7*(1), 1-2.

Crawford, M., and MacLeod, M. 1990. Gender in the college classroom: An assessment of the "chilly climate" for women. *Sex Roles, 23*(3/4), 101-122.

Crawley, A. 2000. Should we act as judge and jury or try to create a culture of academic honesty? *Advocate: For NEA Members in Higher Education*, December, 5-8.

Cronin, T.E. 1992. On celebrating college teaching. *Journal on Excellence in College Teaching*, 3, 149-168.

Cross, K.P. 1986. A proposal to improve teaching, or "what taking teaching seriously should mean." *AAHE Bulletin*, 39(1), 9-15.

Cross, K.P., and Angelo, T.A. 1988. *Classroom Assessment Techniques: A Handbook for Faculty*. Ann Arbor, MI: National Center for Research to Improve Postsecondary Teaching and Learning, University of Michigan.

Cross, K.P. 1997. Developing professional fitness through classroom assessment and classroom research. *The Cross Papers No. 1*. Mission Viejo, CA: League for Innovation in the Community College and Educational Testing Service.

Davis, B.G. 1993. *Tools for Teaching*. San Francisco: Jossey-Bass, Publishers.

Dewey, J. 1963. *Experience and Education*. New York: Collier Books.

Diener, E., Lusk, R., DeFour, D., and Flax, R. 1980. Deindividuation: Effects of group size, density, number of observers, and group member similarity on self-consciousness and disinhibited behavior. *Journal of Personality and Social Psychology*, 39, 449-459.

Eagly, A.H., Makhijani, M.G., and Klonsky, B.G. 1992. Gender and the evaluation of leaders: A meta-analysis. *Psychological Bulletin*, 111, 3-22.

Eagly, A.H., and Mladinic, A. 1994. Are people prejudiced against women? Some answers from research on attitudes, gender stereotypes, and judgments of competence. *European Review of Social Psychology*, 5, 1-35.

Edwards, S., and Bowman, M.A. 1996. Promoting student learning through questioning: A study of classroom questions. *Journal on Excellence in College Teaching*, 7(2), 3-24.

Eison, J.A. 1999. Challenging student passivity. *Advocate: For NEA Members in Higher Education*, February, 6.

Eubanks, I.M. 1991. Nonstandard dialect speakers and collaborative learning. *Writing Instructor*, 10(3), 143-148.

Faust, J.L., and Paulson, D.R. 1998. Active learning in the college classroom. *Journal on Excellence in College Teaching*, 9(2), 3-24.

Fiske, E.B. 1990/April 11. Lessons (a report on research conducted by Catherine G. Krupnick). *The New York Times*, B6.

Fiske, S.T. 1993. Social cognition and social perception. *Annual Review of Psychology*, 44, 155-194.

Frederick, P. 1981. The dreaded discussion: Ten ways to start. *Improving College and University Teaching*, 29(3), 109-114. (Note: This publication is now called *College Teaching*.)

Frost, W.L. 1999. It takes a community to retain a student: The Trinity Law School model. *Journal of College Student Retention: Research, Theory, and Practice*, 1(3) 203-224.

Garko, M., Kough, C., Pignata, G., Kimmel, E.B., and Eison, J. 1994. Myths about student-faculty relationships: What do students really want? *Journal on Excellence in College Teaching*, 5(2), 51-65.

Gillespie, K.H. 1999. Discussion: Alive and well? *Advocate: For NEA Members in Higher Education*, March, 5.

Gullette, M.M. (Ed.). 1984. *The Art and Craft of Teaching*. Cambridge, MA: Harvard University Press.

Goldberg, P.A. 1968. Are women prejudiced against women? *Transactions*, 5, 28-30.Goodkin, V.H. 1982/August. The intellectual consequences of writing: Writing as a tool for learning. Unpublished doctoral dissertation, Rutgers: The State University of New Jersey.

Guskey, T.R. 1988. *Improving Student Learning in College Classrooms*. Springfield, IL: Charles C. Thomas, Publisher.

Hall, R.M., and Sandler, B.R. 1982. The classroom climate: A chilly one for women? *Project on the Status and Education of Women*. Washington, DC: Association of American Colleges.

Haslett, B.J., Geis, F.L., and Carter, M.R. 1992. *The Organizational Woman: Power and Paradox*. Westport, CT: Ablex Publishing.

Heller, J.F., Puff, C.R., and Mills, C.J. 1985. Assessment of the chilly college climate for women. *Journal of Higher Education*, 56(4), 446-461.

Howe, N.H., and Strauss, W. 2000. *Millennials Rising: The Next Great Generation*. New York: Vintage Books.

Hyman, R.T. 1979. *Strategic Questioning*. Englewood Cliffs, NJ: Prentice Hall.

Johnson, D.W., Johnson, R.T., and Smith, K.A. 1991a. *Active Learning: Cooperation in the College Classroom*. Edina, MN: Interaction Book Company.

Johnson, D.W., Johnson, R.T., and Smith, K.A. 1991b. Cooperative learning: Increasing college faculty instructional productivity. *ASHE-ERIC Higher Education Report No. 4*. Washington, DC: George Washington University School of Education and Human Development.

Johnson, E. 1999. Preclude cheating: A response. *The Teaching Professor*, August/September, 5.

Joesting, L.A. (Editor-in-Chief). 1978. *Communicate! A Workbook for Interpersonal Communication*, Second Edition. Dubuque, IA: Kendall/Hunt Publishing Company.

Jordon, L., and Kelly, K. 1990. Effects of academic achievement and gender on academic and social self-concept: A replication study. *Journal of Counseling and Development*, 69, 173-177.

King, A. 1993. From sage on the stage to guide on the side. *College Teaching*, 41(1), 30-35.

Krupnick, C.G. 1993. Meadows College prepares for men. In K. Wilson and M.J. Bane (Eds.), *Gender and Public Policy, Cases and Comments*. Boulder, CO: Westview Press, 137-148.

Krupnick, C.G. 1985. Women and men in the classroom: Inequality and its remedies. *On Teaching and Learning* (Harvard University), 10, 18-25.

Lavoie, R.D. 1989. Understanding learning disabilities: Discussion leader's guide. Accompanying the videotape "How Difficult Can This Be? The F.A.T. City Workshop." Washington, DC: The Learning Project at WETA.

Lefton, L.A. 2000. *Psychology*, Seventh Edition. Needham Heights, MA: Allyn and Bacon.

Light, R.J. 1992. *The Harvard Assessment Seminars*, Second Report. New York: Andrew W. Mellon Foundation.

Magnan, R. 1990. *147 Practical Tips for Teaching Professors*. Madison, WI: Atwood Publishing.

Matlin, M.M. 2000. *The Psychology of Women*, Fourth Edition. Fort Worth, TX: Harcourt College Publishers.

McCabe, D.L., and Pavela, G. 1997. The principled pursuit of academic integrity. *AAHE Bulletin, 50*(4), 11-12.

McGlynn, A.P. 2001/January 8. New semester, new beginnings: Starting the semester with bonding exercises. *Hispanic Outlook, 11*(7), 13-14.

McGlynn, A.P. 2000/March 24. Classroom dynamics and retention: Motivating students to persevere. *Hispanic Outlook, 10*(13), 20-21.

McGlynn, A.P. 2000/October 9. The changing face of the student body: The challenges before us. *Hispanic Outlook, 11*(1), 33-34.

McGlynn, A.P. 2000/September 8. Communication patterns in the classroom: Gender differences, part one. *Hispanic Outlook, 10*(25), 22-24.

McGlynn, A.P. 2000/September 22. Communication patterns in the classroom: Gender differences, part two. *Hispanic Outlook, 10*(26), 16-18.

McKeachie, W.J. 1999. Facilitating discussion: Posing problems, listening, questioning. In W.J. McKeachie (Ed.), *Teaching Tips*, Tenth Edition. Boston: Houghton Mifflin Company, 44-65.

Munde, D. 1999a/April. How to energize your class discussion: In search of critical thinking. *Adjunct Connection News*, 1.

Munde, D. 1999b/October 20. Presentation before Mercer County Community College's Writing Across the Disciplines committee meeting.

Murray, B. 2000. Teaching students how to learn. *Monitor on Psychology, 31*(6), 62-63.

Nygard, J. 1991. Collaborative learning. *Crosstalk: Humanities Division Adjunct Newsletter*, Mercer County Community College, 1.

Office of the Dean for Academic Affairs and Office of the Dean for Student Services, Mercer County Community College. 1996-1998. *How to Succeed at Mercer: A Do-It-Yourself Guide to Effective Study Skills*. Trenton, NJ: Office of the Dean for Academic Affairs and the Office of the Dean for Student Services, Mercer County Community College.

Padilla, R.V. 1999. College student retention: Focus on success. *Journal of College Student Retention: Research, Theory, and Practice, 1*(2), 131-146.

Parker, R.P., and Goodkin, V. 1987. *The Consequences of Writing: Enhancing Learning in the Disciplines*. Portsmouth, NH: Boynton/Cook and Heinemann Educational Books.

Parry, S. 1990. Feminist pedagogy. In E. Hedges, M.M. Goldberg, and S. Coulter (Eds.), *Community College Guide to Curriculum Change*. Towson State University and Maryland Community College, FIPSE PROJECT (Fund for the Improvement of Post Secondary Education, U.S. Department of Education).

Paul, E. 1999/April 21. "Challenging Student Passivity and Resistance to Learning." Workshop presented at Mercer County Community College.

Penfield, J. 1998. *Respecting Diversity, Working for Equity: A Handbook for Trainers*. Arlington, MA: Joyce Penfield Associates.

Perlman, B., and McCann, L.I. 1998. Students' pet peeves about teaching. *Teaching of Psychology, 25*, 201-202.

Piaget, J. 1952. *The Origins of Intelligence in Children*, M. Cook (Trans.). New York: International Universities Press.

Pintrich, P.R. 1995. *Understanding Self-Regulated Learning. New Directions for Teaching and Learning, 63*. San Francisco: Jossey-Bass, Publishers.

Prentice-Dunn, S., and Rogers, R.W. 1989. Deindividuation and the self-regulation of behavior. In P.B. Paulus (Ed.), *Psychology of Group Influence*, Second Edition. Hillsdale, NJ: Lawrence Erlbaum Associates, 87-109.

Public Broadcasting Service. 1999/April 8. "Faculty on the Front Lines: Reclaiming Civility in the Classroom." Videoconference produced by Dallas Teleconferences, Dallas TeleLearning, LeCroy Center for Educational Telecommunications, and Dallas County Community College District.

Richardson, S.M. 2000. Civility: What went wrong? *Advocate: For NEA Members in Higher Education*, March, 5-8.

Richardson, S.M. (Ed.). 1999. *Promoting Civility: A Teaching Challenge. New Directions for Teaching and Learning, 77*. San Francisco: Jossey-Bass, Publishers.

Rose, A.J., and Montemayor, R. 1994. The relationship between gender role orientation and perceived self-competency in male and female adolescents. *Sex Roles, 31*(9/10), 579-595.

Rosenthal, N. 1990. Active learning/empowered learning. *Adult Learning, 1*(5), 16-18.

Rowe, M.P. 1977. The Saturn's rings phenomenon: Micro-inequities and unequal opportunity in the American economy. In P. Bourne and V. Parness (Eds.), *Proceedings: National Science Foundation Conference on Women's Leadership and Authority*. Santa Cruz, CA: University of California-Santa Cruz.

Rutgers University. 1989. *Training of Trainers Multicultural/Multiracial Development Program*. Alamont, NY: DeLoayza Associates.

Sacks, P. 1996. *Generation X Goes to College: An Eye-Opening Account of Teaching in Postmodern America*. Peru, IL: Open Court Publishing Company.

Sadker, M., and Sadker, D. 1994. *Failing at Fairness: How America's Schools Cheat Girls*. New York: C. Scribner's Sons.

Sadker, M., and Sadker, D. 1990. Confronting sexism in the college classroom. In S.L. Gabriel and I Smithson (Eds.), *Gender in the Classroom: Power and Pedagogy*. Urbana, IL: University of Illinois Press, 176-187.

References

Sandler, B.R., and Hoffman, E. 1992. *Teaching Faculty Members to be Better Teachers: A Guide to Equitable and Effective Classroom Techniques*. Washington, DC: Association of American Colleges.

Sandler, B.R., Silverberg, L.A., and Hall, R.M. 1996. *The Chilly Classroom Climate: A Guide to Improve the Education of Women*. Washington, DC: National Association for Women in Education.

Schneider, A. 1998. Insubordination and intimidation signal the end of decorum in many classrooms. *The Chronicle of Higher Education*, March 27, A12-A14.

Sheridan, J., Byrne, A.C., and Quina, K. 1989. Collaborative learning: Notes from the field. *College Teaching*, 37(2), 49-53.

Sherif, M., Harvey, O.J., White, B.J., Hood, W., and Sherif, C. 1961. *Intergroup Conflict and Cooperation: The Robber's Cave Experiment*. Norman, OK: Institute of Intergroup Relations, University of Oklahoma.

Silberman, M. 1996. *Active Learning: 101 Strategies to Teach Any Subject*. Needham Heights, MA: Allyn and Bacon.

Slavin, R.E. 1997. *Educational Psychology: Theory and Practice*, Fifth Edition. Needham Heights, MA: Allyn and Bacon.

Springer, L., Stanne, M.E., and Donovan, S.S. 1998. *Effects of Small-Group Learning on Undergraduates in Science, Mathematics, Engineering, and Technology: A Meta-Analysis*. Madison, WI: National Institute for Science Education.

Stein, J.A., Newcomb, M.D., and Bentler, P.M. 1992. The effect of agency and communality on self-esteem: Gender differences in longitudinal data. *Sex Roles*, 26(11/12), 465-483.

Stock, G. 1987. *The Book of Questions*. New York: Workman Publishing.

Swim, J., Borgida, E., Maruyama, G., and Myers, D.G. 1989. Joan McKay versus John McCay: Do gender stereotypes bias evaluations? *Psychological Bulletin*, 105(3), 409-429.

Tinto, V. 1998. Colleges as communities: Taking research on student persistence seriously. *The Review of Higher Education*, 21(2), 167-177.

Turner, R.C. 1999. Adapting to a new generation of college students. *Thought and Action*. 15(2), 33-42.

Unger, R.K. 1988. Psychological, feminist, and personal epistemology: Transcending contradiction. In M.M. Gergen (Ed.), *Feminist Thought and the Structure of Knowledge*. New York: New York University Press, 124-141.

Valde, G.A. 1997. Promoting student participation and learning through the use of weekly writing assignments. *Journal on Excellence in College Teaching*, 8(3), 67-76.

VanZile-Tamsen, C., and Livingston, J.A. 1999. The differential impact of motivation on the self-regulated strategy use of high- and low-achieving college students. *Journal of College Student Development*, 40(1), 54-60.

Wagener, U., and Nettles, M. 1998. It takes a community to educate students: How three HBCUFEE's succeed at retention. *Change: The Magazine of Higher Learning*, 30(2), 18-25.

Wiener, H.S. 1986. Collaborative learning in the classroom: A guide to evaluation. *College English, 48*(1), 52-61.

Weinstein, C.E., and Hume, L.M. 1998. *Study Strategies for Lifelong Learning.* Washington, DC: American Psychological Association.

Welty, W.M. 1989. Discussion method teaching. *Change: The Magazine of Higher Learning*, July/August, 40-49.

Widaman, K.F. et al. 1992. Differences in adolescents' self-concept as a function of academic level, ethnicity, and gender. *American Journal on Mental Retardation, 96*(4), 387-403.

Wilgoren, J. 2000. Swell of minority students is predicted at colleges. *The New York Times*, May 24, A14.

Wilkinson, J., and Ansell, H. 1992. Introduction. *On Teaching and Learning* (Harvard University), 4, 4.

Wolcowitz, J. 1984. The first day of class. In M.M. Gullette (Ed.), *The Art and Craft of Teaching*. Cambridge, MA: Harvard University Press, 10-24.

Worell, J. 1989. Sex roles in transition. In J. Worell and F. Danner (Eds.), *The Adolescent as Decision-Maker: Applications to Development and Education*. San Diego: Academic Press, 245-280.

Zimbardo, P.G. 1970. The human choice: Individuation, reason, and order versus deindividuation, impulse, and chaos. In W.J. Arnold and D. Levine (Eds.), *Nebraska Symposium on Motivation, 17*, 237-307.

Zimmerman, B. 1998. Academic studying and the development of personal skill: A self-regulatory perspective. *Educational Psychologist, 33*(2/3), 73-86.

# About the Author

Angela Provitera McGlynn is a Professor of Psychology at Mercer County Community College (MCCC) in West Windsor, New Jersey, where she has been teaching for thirty years. She is the co-author (with Florence Rhyn Serlin) of *Living with Yourself, Living with Others: A Woman's Guide* (Prentice-Hall 1979). She is also the author of three books published by MCCC: *Celebrating Diversity: Enhancing Harmony on Campus* (1990), *Teaching Tips: Improving College Instruction* (1992), and *Classroom Atmosphere in College: Improving the Teaching/Learning Environment* (1996). In addition, she has written numerous journal articles on a wide range of topics, presented workshops across the United States, and appeared on radio and national television programs.